Your Unfinished Life...

LAWRENCE J. DANKS

© Copyright 2009, Lawrence J. Danks

All rights reserved

No part of this book may be reproduced, stored in a retrieval system, or transmitted by any means, electronic, mechanical, photocopying, recording, or otherwise, without written permission from the author.

ISBN: 978-0-615-24207-1

Contents

Chapter 1	Kindness and Happiness	7
Chapter 2	On Kindness [1911]	25
Chapter 3	Kindness [1892]	47
Chapter 4	Finding Yourself Through Others	77
Chapter 5	Conflicting Thoughts On Kindness	93
Chapter 6	You Can Make A Difference	105
Chapter 7	40 Ways To Be Kind	113
Chapter 8	Make Someone Happy - And You Will Be Happy Too	149
Chapter 9	Concluding Thoughts on Finding Happiness	157

For my parents,
Margaret and Thomas J. Danks
who lived lives of kindness

For those I will always love,
For all those who have been kind to me,
For those who need kindness,
For those who extend it
For everyone else who can

Chapter 1

Kindness and Happiness

"People often asked me what is the most effective technique for transforming their life. It is a little embarrassing that after years and years of research and experimentation, I have to say that the best answer is - just be a little kinder."- [Aldous Huxley -Quoted from *The Power of Kindness* - Piero Ferrucci]

The search for happiness is a universal quest. It seems only logical it should center around us. Instead, it really centers around others. As English philosopher and social reformer Jeremy Bentham said: "Create all the happiness you can create, remove all the misery you can remove. Every day will allow you to add something to the pleasure of others, or to diminish something of their pains. And for every grain of enjoyment you sow in the bosom of another, you shall find a harvest in your own bosom; while every sorrow which you pluck out from the thoughts and feelings of a fellow creature shall be replaced by a beautiful peace and joy in the sanctuary of your soul." - [Quoted from *Happiness: Lessons From A New Science* - Richard Layard]

How often are people called to our attention and we think that somebody else will help or that it's not really our concern? It can be as simple as giving or lending money, cutting someone's grass or listening to a friend's problems.

A decent, thoughtful man was walking home late one night and saw a pathetic drunk laying in the gutter. Suddenly, he found himself under a horrific attack of cynical thought and said to himself: "God, why do you let this man lie in shame. If you truly exist, why don't you help him?" And into this man's mind came this sentence: "I am helping him. I just brought him to your attention." - [*Power Thoughts*- Robert Schuller]

Opportunities for kindness present themselves daily. By developing an enhanced sensitivity to our social environment, we'll notice things we haven't seen before. More people will be helped. And we'll make ourselves more authentic and happier people in the process.

How To Have A Happier Life

You are the prospective parent of your own fulfilled self and your happiness. Dr. Martin Seligman, Professor of Psychology at the University of Pennsylvania, in his book *Authentic Happiness* says this about true happiness:

"The pleasant life, is wrapped up in the successful pursuit of positive feelings, supplemented by the skills of amplifying these emotions. The good life, in contrast, is not about maximizing positive emotion, but is a life wrapped up in successfully using 'signature strengths' to obtain abundant and authentic gratification. The meaningful life has one additional feature: "using your signature strengths in the service of something larger than you are."

Mother Teresa was of the same mind: "I wouldn't touch a leper for $1000, but I cure him willingly for the love of God." It doesn't necessarily have to do with God or religious faith. It simply has to do with doing something worthwhile for a higher purpose.

Benjamin Disraeli, former Prime Minister of Great Britain, who as a Jew faced great religious and ethnic discrimination, rose to the top by "climbing the greasy pole" as he described it. He noted: "Life is to short to be little". We should focus on doing important things. How big or little is your life? What else could you be doing that is truly important to you? By changing our focus, we can change our life.

Students in Dr. Seligman's classes wondered if happiness came more readily by extending a kindness or by having fun. They were asked to engage in one pleasurable activity and one activity involved with helping others. Dr. Seligman reported that "the pleasurable activity paled in comparison with the effects of the kind action." Kindness or service is not the sole road to gratification, but it clearly meets the standards of being an important source of it.

To determine what your own personal strengths are, read *Authentic Happiness* and take Dr. Seligman's VIA Strengths Survey. A version of the test is also available online at *www.authentichappiness.org*. Reading his book will provide an improved understanding of your strengths and how they may be best applied in leading you to a happier and more satisfying life.

Take the long term view. Robert Schuller said that we should plan as if we are going to live to be one hundred.

Whether we get there or not, having a plan will help us maximize what we're going to accomplish in whatever time we have left.

Kindness As A Strength

Kindness is an important strength all of us can practice. It allows us to focus on something outside ourselves, something larger than we are. Being kind usually isn't difficult. It requires no special training or equipment. It only requires attentiveness and willingness to help.

While sixty, seventy or eighty years of life may seem like a long time, time for all of us is finite. Joel Osteen, pastor of the Lakewood Church in Houston notes: "Life is a mist. We're here for a moment. Then we're gone...Don't just make a living. Make a life." We have limited control over how long we live, but we have a great deal of control over how we live.

Our own life, when compared against the expanse of eternity and the generations that have preceded us, is startlingly short, but nevertheless it can be productive. How productive have we been so far? How meaningful are we going to be in the time we have left? Are we going to leave a legacy worth remembering? Maria Shriver puts a fine point on it in *And One More Thing Before You Go*: "You want to feel good? Then do good." Joel Osteen mirrors that thought in his self-help book, *Your Best Life Now*: "You will never be truly fulfilled as a human being, until you learn the simple secret of how to give your life away."

Kindness produces insight and creates an improved sense of self-worth. Get to know the real you. As James Hollis says in *Finding Meaning in the Second Half of Life*: "Deconstruct the false self...Live your life to produce greater substance...Don't be afraid to be who you really are. Don't be a false self. Be authentic."

Many self-help books, including the blockbuster best seller *A New Earth: Awakening to Your Life's Purpose* by Eckhart Tolle, have emphasized the importance of living in the present moment because that's also where our future lies. All of us should be challenged by "the fierce urgency of now" to produce the positive change in our lives that Martin Luther King spoke of in a different context.

Touchstones of Kindness

How do we know what to do and when to act? Jean Guibert in his insightful work, *On Kindness*, provides a memorable guide for kindness when he says, "wherever there is misery, there it speeds."

Your Unfinished Life provides commentary on two classic, and largely long lost works: Jean Guibert's *On Kindness* and Frederick Faber's *Kindness*. Guibert was a French priest. His inspiring words are his legacy. Faber was a British priest and poet, best known as a hymn writer. Kindness is a major avenue toward happiness. These highly perceptive works provide guidance and sensitivity on how to best extend it, and even when it might be a kindness not to extend one. It might seem as if no one would need a "how to" guide for extending kindness, but you may agree after reading their words, that it can only be improved by implementing their insightful recommendations.

Some readers may become a bit impatient with the slower pace as they read through these two chapters, but the wisdom contained in their writings is both affecting and timeless and is well worth the trek. They provide a great treasury of thoughts for reflection. They also contain charming language from a time gone by. No one could read these summaries without seeing themselves and others in them. They will speak to you in magical and eloquent ways that I never could.

It might seem as if kindness just operates by instinct. Often it does. But like many other things in life, some guidance can be helpful in producing better results. A principal purpose of this book is to selectively bring some of the beautiful thoughts from these works to the light of day again. They were deemed necessary by their authors a century ago when times were far simpler. How much more must they be needed today?

Since Fathers Guibert and Faber came from a Roman Catholic tradition, not unsurprisingly God is mentioned in their writings. Their books are about doing good and extending kindness. This book isn't intended as a religious book. It's goal is to be inspirational and spiritual in a broader sense. Its principles are applicable to all people of any faith, or of none.

Their thoughts have been supplemented by excerpts from Marcus Aurelius' *Meditations* on living a worthwhile life, by the insightful words of Mother Teresa, and by the quotations of many other wise observers as diverse as The Dalai Lama and George Foreman.

You probably haven't always been kind. I certainly haven't. I've done some unkind and insensitive things, sometimes out of thoughtlessness, other times out of selfishness or immaturity. Other times there were omissions, things in retrospect I wish I had done, but didn't do.

Kindness never ceases to be a challenge. It is far easier to talk about and write about, than it is to extend it. Famed opera singer Beverly Sills said we should all ask ourselves: "How do you take a life and make something of it?" An answer Gandhi proposed was to "be the change you want to see in the world."

Moving Your Life In The Right Direction

We all have something to give, whether it's time, money, expertise or other gifts. It may be helpful to imitate the example of others, but the best gifts we can give are uniquely ours, as the following tale suggests: Joseph, a Jewish man, goes to heaven and meets St. Peter. Joseph says to him: "Tell God I wish I had been like Moses or Abraham. God told Peter to say to him: "Tell him I'm sorry he wasn't more like Joseph." Model after others if it motivates you, but be uniquely yourself.

We should give as often as we can. For some of us it will be frequently, for others only occasionally. It all helps. It might take us a while to get there, but as with any other worthwhile direction we're moving in, we don't always have to be running or walking toward it. It's ok to crawl sometimes too.

When done frequently enough, it might allow us to gain the same surprising insight that Walt Whitman did: "I am larger, better than I thought. I did not know I held so much goodness." In *The Power of Kindness,* Piero Ferrucci similarly states: "I did not know I had inside me, like everyone, so many precious goods. When we can live this revelation, it not only helps others, it can help us discover what's missing in our own lives." There is always time. As the highly talented actor Sally Field remarked: "It's never too late to become who you might have been."

Stephen Covey, in his best selling book, *The Seven Habits of Highly Successful People*, mentions a story about two men standing by the casket of a deceased friend. One said to the other: "How much did he leave?" His friend said: "He left it all." No matter how wonderful something tangible is, you can't take it with you.

In a material and self-absorbed society, it's easy to focus on ourselves and our own egos. Marcus Aurelius' *Meditations* furnishes us with a vivid perspective on the folly of self-absorbed acquisition and of manufactured self-importance: "All things fade into the storied past, and in a little while are shrouded in oblivion. Even to men whose lives were a blaze of glory this comes to pass; as to the rest, the breath is hardly out of them before, in Homer's words: "they are lost to sight and hearsay alike."

Take it from someone who grew up in a funeral home, truer words were never spoken. A pensive walk through any cemetery reminds us that regarding anything of the world, it all comes to a screeching halt at a piece of stone and a small patch of earth, even for the wealthiest, most glorious and egocentric among us. But what then is lasting? All we can really take with us is the good we've done for others.

This obituary appeared in *The New York Times* on Sunday, September 15, 2002: "Salvatore Altchek, 'the $5 Doctor' of Brooklyn, Dies at 92." He saw patients until two months before his death. He gave up house calls, which he made on foot at 87, and charged $5 or $10, or nothing at all. One woman said: "He wasn't out to make money; he was out to help people." Another said: "He is a physician who treated the poor [as well as lawyers and longshoremen], and never asked for money from the oppressed community. They paid him when they had it, and he treated them as if they were Park Avenue residents. For more than fifty years, he began his workday at 8AM, took half an hour off for dinner at 5PM and closed the office door at 8. He then made house calls, often until midnight." Most of us can't be physicians, but all of us can be Dr. Altcheks by following his example.

Writer Charlotte Forten pondered: "I wonder why it is I have this strange feeling of not living out myself." Have you ever had this feeling? That part of you is missing? That you're not fully being who you really are?

Joseph Campbell, the famed lecturer and writer tells us: "The banality of our current life is always waiting to yield a greater story…Too many of us accept the sadness of inauthentic lives…The best way to help mankind is the perfection of yourself." This book is about trying to authenticate lives, yours and mine, through kindness and the creation of happiness. As playwright Arthur Miller said, reflecting on the inspiration that spawned the Brooklyn Bridge: "You too might add something that could last and be beautiful."

The End Game

The Dalai Lama, remarking on the role of kindness in life said: "My religion is very simple: my key motivation is love. My religion is kindness…All religions [and the ethics of any good person] share a common root, which is limitless compassion. They emphasize human improvement, love, respect for others and compassion for the suffering of others. Insofar as love is essential in every religion, we could say that love is a universal religion." [*The Dalai Lama's Little Book of Inner Peace*]

In the French film, *The Barbarian Invasions*, a dying man, who led a selfish life, searches for meaning in his final days. Near the end, he thinks of himself as a failure. He says he wants "to leave a mark, so I can die in peace."

What mark will you leave? Will you die with the peace you want? What is the meaning of life after all? It's the meaning we decide to give it. Deathbed enlightenments, like the one in this film are better than none, but they're hardly a substitute for a valued life, well lived. We may not achieve all the success and happiness we seek, but we certainly don't want to die a failure because we never tried either. This book is all about making the attempt.

After composer Gustav Mahler died, admirers sent a funeral wreath which read: "Bereft of the saintly human being Gustav Mahler, we are left forever with a never to be lost example of his life and impact." It would be a nice epitaph to work toward - although some of us might have to leave the saintly part off .

Former President Jimmy Carter noted in his excellent book *Living Faith*:

"The most unforgettable funeral I ever attended, maybe with the exception of my own family members, was the service for Mrs. Martin Luther King Sr., mother of the nation's greatest civil rights leader...The Reverend Otis Moss from Cleveland, Ohio preached a brief, but remarkable, sermon about 'the little dash in between' [on a grave stone, the dash between the year someone was born and the year he/she died]...He said everybody has what might be called 'a little dash' to us, but with God, it is everything. The question

Kindness and Happiness

is what do we do with that little dash in between, which represents our life on earth... We have to remember that our lives will become shrunken, if we act only from a cautious sense of duty. It is the reaching, the inspiration, the extra commitment that provides the foundation for a full and gratifying life. After we satisfy all our personal needs and desires, then what? It is not through gratifying our physical needs that we find our purpose in life. We shouldn't carry around what we are in a closed jar and use a medicine dropper to expend it. The little dash in between can be a glorious experience."

If you're not satisfied with the quality of your own contribution at this point, there's still time left to do something about it. As Wayne Dyer commented: "You can't be concerned about the wake your boat has left so far. All you can do is to propel yourself forward with kindness to make some difference now." - [*10 Secrets For Success and Inner Peace*]

There's still lots of time left for most of us to do many things to benefit others, by words, actions or example, whether we're living an active daily life, or leading a circumscribed existence caused by the care of children or of a family member, illness, advanced age, imprisonment or other circumstances.

Finding success in life can sometimes be elusive. *The Seven Habits of High Successful People* offers a well-structured plan to get there. A basic step is to define what success and happiness mean to us. One suggestion Stephen Covey offers is to write your own eulogy. What would you want people to say about you after you're gone? Then using those benchmarks, guide your life. Naturally, you can change them any time you want, but they can provide a solid basis for making life decisions and for focusing your efforts in the proper direction. On the lists of many people would be the goal of "doing something worthwhile" or of "making a difference." *Your Unfinished Life* examines kindness and offers help and encouragement to guide you along your path to fulfillment and happiness. "We get to discover how much of us is lead and how much is gold. Like the alchemist, we get a chance to turn lead into gold by our own thoughts, words and actions." - [*A Short Course on Kindness* - Margot Silk Forrest]

The Challenge Of Everyday Life

Sometimes truths are right in front of us, but are obscured by our daily routines, by work, or by raising and supporting a family. Just being too busy with life. Eventually, we learn many truths through experience, reading, the passage of time and reflection: "The quieter you become, the more you can hear" – Baba Ram Dass.

Not only is it a challenge to be kind, it is also one to avoid being unkind. When we're quieter we can recognize that: "By far the greater part of violence that humans have inflicted on each other is not the work of criminals or the mentally deranged, but of normal, respectable citizens in service of the collective ego." - [*A New Earth* - Eckhart Tolle]

It's taken me almost sixty-four years to get this far. I wish it hadn't taken so long. Maybe some of this will help you learn some of these priceless truths faster than I did.

Actor Naomi Watts, in an interview with James Lipton for the insightful interview program "The Actor's Studio", said she was an assistant fashion editor when she decided to take a weekend acting class. During the weekend she said she realized: "I'm living a lie. This is what matters to me." Afterward, she quit her fashion job to focus on acting.

We might not exactly be living a lie, although some of us may be, but we might not exactly be living the full truth either. When we give our life some thought and learn to be kinder, we'll not only find out what matters to us, but we'll also get to know the fuller truth about ourselves. It can bring a lot more happiness to ourselves and to others as a result. "What you give is yours for good. What you keep is lost forever." - [From the French film, *Monsieur Ibrahim*]

Stairway to Happiness

Time Magazine in "The New Science of Happiness" reported that happiness is based on gratitude and kindness. Based on her research findings and those of others, Stanford University psychologist Sonja Lyubomirsky cited eight steps toward a more satisfying life:

1. Count your blessings
2. Practice acts of kindness
   "These should be both random [letting a harried mom go ahead in the checkout line] and systematic [bringing Sunday dinner to an elderly neighbor]. Being kind to others, whether friends or strangers, triggers a cascade of positive effects. It makes you feel generous and capable, gives you a greater sense of connection with others and wins you smiles, approval, and reciprocated kindness – all happiness boosters."
3. Savor life's joys
4. Thank a mentor

5. Learn to forgive
6. Invest time and energy in friends and family
7. Take care of your body
    "Getting plenty of sleep, exercising, stretching, smiling and laughing all enhance your mood in the short term."
8. Develop strategies for dealing with stress and hardships. Religious faith has been shown to help people cope, but so do secular beliefs enshrined in axioms like "This too shall pass" and "That which doesn't kill me makes me stronger." The trick is you have to believe them.

Danger: Do Not Enter

Life passes through stages. The latter stages of life have some marked differences from earlier years. James Hollis in his book, *Finding Meaning in the Second Half of Life: How To Really Grow Up*, quotes Carl Jung with his advice on how to stay away from trouble: "I have frequently seen people when they content themselves with inadequate or wrong answers to the questions of life. They seek position, marriage, reputation, outward success or money, and remain unhappy and neurotic, even when they attain what they are seeking. Such people are usually contained within too narrow a spiritual horizon. Their life has not sufficient content, sufficient meaning. [What Joseph Campbell called 'climbing ladders in life, only to find out later that they were placed against the wrong walls.'] If they are enabled to develop into more spacious personalities, the neurosis generally disappears."

Hollis says: "We need to be strong enough to examine our lives and to make risky changes." Many of those changes can involve risk, but not all of them. Extending kindness usually involves little or no risk, yet helps satisfy the prescription Hollis advocates: "The ego's highest task is to go beyond itself into service, service to what is really desired by the soul, rather than the complex-ridden ego or the values of the culture." Hollis' excellent book is a thoughtful and challenging tool that can help you move toward finding a higher and better self.

Self-Evaluation and Completion

How will we know when we have done enough to find happiness and to bring it to others? We can answer by asking: What does it take for you to be proud of who you are? As Richard Bach wrote so poignantly in *Jonathan Livingston Seagull*: "How will I know when I have completed my mission?" The answer: "If you are still breathing, you are not done."

There is no heavier burden than a great or unused potential. Rocky Balboa in *Rocky 6*, asks himself if he "still has anything left in the basement." As we grow older, most of us may ask ourselves similar questions, and also the one Private Ryan did at the graveside of his rescuer, at the end of the gripping film *Saving Private Ryan* : "Have I been a good man [woman]?" *Your Unfinished Life* will help you make a difference, help you feel happier about yourself, and help you find more contentment at the end of your life, so you can answer that question with confidence and peace.

Randy Pausch, the well known former professor from Carnegie-Mellon, who facing imminent death, said in his famous book *The Last Lecture*: "I have a chance here to really think about what matters most to me, to cement how people will remember me, and to do whatever good I can on the way out." Like Randy Pausch was, we are all on the way out too. He just had a better idea of when. As one of his doctors told him: "It's important to behave as if you're going to be around for a while." That's great advice for us too because most of us are going to be.

Clarifications

Any parenthetical text and italicizations for emphasis throughout the book are mine. Quotations have been identified by author whenever possible.

Headings have been added and some modifications have been made to the excerpts from the original works of Fathers Guibert and Faber to improve clarity and readability. Since these works were written many years ago, the authors use the word "man" when referring to what would more appropriately be referred to today as humankind, or just more simply, people. Clearly, their thoughts were directed to both women and men. You may also note that my coverage of the later work precedes the earlier one. It seemed more important to go from a generalized view to a more specific view, than to necessarily present those works in chronological order.

Extracting The Essentials

I would highly recommend reading this book with a highlighter or pen in hand to mark off passages and quotations that are particularly meaningful to you. It will save having to hunt through the entire book when you're trying to find something later.

"When we live without meaning,
we suffer the greatest illness of all."
Finding Meaning In The Second Half Of Life - James Hollis

"Success rests with having the courage and the endurance and, above all, the will to become the person you are, however peculiar that may be. Then you will be able to say: "I have found my hero and he is me."
– George Sheehan

Chapter 2

On Kindness [1911]

Jean Guibert

[*On Kindness* is a small book I found among my mother's personal effects after she died. After many years, it started me on the path of writing this book. A selected summary of it, with my parenthetical comments, appears below. It's style is simple, humble and affectingly beautiful.]

Preface

No duty do we require to be more frequently reminded of than that of being kind. Just as men long for others to be kind to them, so they are slow to grow in this virtue, and remiss in its practice. It is so important to stir up in ourselves the instinctive kindness... implanted in the depths of every human soul, but which too often is stifled out by a life of selfishness.

The Exceeding Worth of Kindness

Kindness Is A Virtue of Great Price

Kindness is to be felt rather than to be defined. It is better to experience it, than to try to explain what it is. Moreover, its home is in the heart, rather than in the intellect.

Sometimes it takes the form of a special affection, manifesting itself by gentleness, affability, obligingness, amiability and graciousness. Sometimes it takes a more active form, inspiring zeal, generosity, devotedness and self-denial. But oftener it is externally, hardly more than passive, enabling the kind man to practice patience and endurance, to be indulgent and sympathetic with others, to forgive injuries, and to humbly forget himself.

Kindness is a retiring virtue ... in silence and in the dark it does good and therewith is content... that kindness is prone to conceal itself takes nothing from its worth.

All Men Love The Kind-Hearted

Father Faber remarks: "Kindness makes life bearable." Under this cross some fall to rise no more, others march bravely onwards. Why this difference? May it not be that some lose heart because they know not how to hope? Others, their hearts enlarged by happiness, are rushed on by the very joy of their being. Of a truth, facing life, man is strong or weak accordingly, as he is cheerful or sad at heart. Sadness quenches the living fire within him, happiness is as fuel to it. And what breath better than that of a kindness received, to fan the flames of joy in a man's heart?

On Kindness [1911]Jean Guibert

Kindness Overcomes All Things

The double reward of kind words is the happiness they cause in others, and the happiness they cause in ourselves... It is because a man feels that he is and ought to be free that he hates to yield to force, but gives way easily to kindness. We could soothe many sufferings if, as St. Francis de Sales has told us to do, we made kindness "the first dressing for the wounds which we undertake to heal." Victor Hugo's maxim applies: "If you want to make men better, make them happier." [Victor Hugo(1802-1885) was an important French novelist and dramatist. His best-known works were *Les Miserables* and *The Hunchback of Notre Dame*.]

St. Vincent de Paul said,

"The very convicts amongst who I lived can be gained over by kindness, and in no other way. When I spoke harshly to them I spoilt everything, and on the contrary, when I praised them for being resigned to their hard lot and pitied their sufferings; when I...showed them that I felt for them, then they listened to me..." [St. Vincent de Paul(1581-1660) was born and died in France. He served as a parish priest in Paris starting organizations to help the poor, to nurse the sick and to find jobs for the unemployed.]

And that angelic soul, Madame Swetchine, who by her shear force of kindness ruled so many, expresses herself admirably: "If good people were kinder people, there would not be so many sinners." [Madame Swetchine(1782-1857) was born in Moscow. She settled in Paris and maintained a salon renowned for its intellectual brilliance and religious atmosphere.]

The conclusion we may put is St. John Chrysostom's:

"Throw the net of charity, bait it with kindness. Remain always a lamb and you will always be a conqueror." [St. John Chrysostom was the Patriarch of Constantinople and a renowned speaker.]

In setting forth the excellency of kindness we have shown that alone it makes the kind man perfectly happy, that alone it conquers the souls of men...Truly Montaigne was right when he insisted that "every other science is hurtful to him who is not well versed in the science of goodwill to his fellow-men." And with him we may add: "Even if I could make myself feared, I had far rather make myself loved." [Michel Eyquem Seigneur de Montaigne(1533-1592) was a famous French essayist.]

On The Nature Of True Kindness

The first of all acts of kindness is to pity any who suffer: a heart moved by the pain of another straightaway feels itself instantly drawn to succor him in his trouble. But the gifts of the kind man must be given kindly and graciously, or else the act will be no balm to the soul of the sufferer.

True Kindness Is Compassionate

There are men and women who take no note of the sufferings of others. Every day they see people in trouble; but it neither surprises them nor affects them...They simply pass on, nor allow the trouble of their neighbor to draw them for a single instant from the pursuit of their pleasure or from their business. Nothing will they sacrifice for the sake of their fellow-creatures. It is such as these one is thinking, when one speaks of hard, cold, callous hearts.

There are men and women who, in the presence of acute

distress, forget to pity the sufferer, so intent are they on discovering where the fault lies. They seem to be seeking to know the truth, in order that they may feel justified in shutting compassionateness out of their hearts and in trampling on those who have fallen, rather than reaching out to them with a helping hand; they have made known weaknesses of others about which they would do well to be silent and take a truly criminal pleasure in fatally compromising, by their indiscreet utterances, persons whom a charitable silence might have saved. ["Gossiping often carries an element of malicious criticism and judgment of others, and so it also strengthens the ego through the implied moral superiority that is there whenever a negative judgment is applied to someone...Whenever you feel superior to anyone, that's the ego in you." (*The New Earth* - Eckhart Tolle.) He advises that as long as our egos predominate, personal growth will be stalled.]

The impulses of a kind heart are quite other. By a mysterious instinct it seems to be conscious of distress; no detail of pain escapes it, it pierces any and every poor cloak with which shame may seek to hide its wretchedness. He does not trouble to blame the unfortunate; he knows only how to commiserate with them, to suffer with them and most of all to understand them. ["Far from turning away from the sight of suffering as from something that revolts, the man of kind heart cannot refrain from gazing upon what only makes him long the more to stay and help." - Mother Teresa]

For him, a fault is atoned for by the mere fact that it is suffered for. Indeed a true heart cannot heed the fault; it sees only the consequent misery; and this is the very reason why the pity of the truly kindhearted is so sweet to all who mourn.

To the kind man every sort of trouble appeals: bodily pain, sadness of heart, the wounds one's surroundings or one's bad fortune have inflicted, and mental suffering—for surely the pain of the mind is the hardest of all to bear.

The kind man never makes little of another's real sufferings... He concerns himself too, about all sorts of distress which people, as a rule, do not trouble themselves...Secretly the kind heart feeds the shamefaced poor; very noticeably it shows respect for and honors all whom the world scorns; on the forsaken and the desolate it lavishes its words of comfort and encouragement...Nor can there ever be a lack of opportunities for the kind heart to show itself as such.

The compassionate heart never wearies; day after day distress appeals to it, moves it - as if there were always novelty in pain. It is attracted by suffering, not from reason or duty, nor because it has made a business of charity, not even to fulfill the will of God – high as this last motive is – but because it is a human being that suffers.

Lacordaire said: "Kindness is a virtue that does not think about its own interest; does not wait for the call of duty; has no need of aesthetic attraction to solicit it; but is instinctively the more drawn towards its object, the more that object is wretched, poor, forsaken, and humanly speaking, contemptible ...God's mercy is for the merciful, and for the merciful alone." [Jean Baptiste Henri Dominique Lacordaire(1802-1861) was a great orator and writer of the 19th century.]

On Kindness [1911] Jean Guibert

True Kindness Is Generous

"Good impulses are just nothing at all, unless they develop into good actions." This remark of a thinker is not altogether true, for the mere pity felt by a kind heart may be itself a kind deed. All sufferers are helped by feeling themselves understood, thought about and sympathized with...Tears of sympathy are never shed in vain; they heal the wounds that caused them to flow.

But to pity is, after all, only to begin to do good; of its very nature kindness tends to express itself by means of kind and charitable actions....Father Faber has very truly laid down that: "Kindness is the overflowing of self upon others." To still the cry of pain, it sacrifices everything—time, money, trouble, its very existence.

Kindness Delayed, Kindness Denied

The compassionate heart gives of its time.

[My father was an exemplary parent to my sister and me, a gentle and kindly man, admired by everyone who knew him. I would occasionally mention to him something I was thinking about doing to help someone. In trying to encourage me to act, rather than just talking about it, he would mention the old axiom that: "The road to hell is paved with good intentions."

I was having a conversation with a fine and highly accomplished gentleman who teaches on our college faculty. I mentioned this expression to him, relevant to something we were discussing at the time. He said he had never heard it before. He laughed and said that his father had always expressed a similar sentiment to him in India as a boy: "If you are thinking about doing something good, do it before you count to three."

I thought it was such wise advice. How often do we think about doing something kind, then just put it off? I once had a relative who was in the hospital. I intended to go visit him, but kept putting it off. He died before I got around to going. Like a goaltender who fails to block a shot, there are occasions in life when you don't get a second chance. Since then, I've tried to act more promptly in similar situations to avoid making that mistake again.

Appreciation and kindness should never go unextended, particularly because of poor time management or laziness. How much more good would be done in the world if people just acted on good impulses immediately? When we think about doing something kind, it's better to just call or e-mail, make the visit, send the money, whatever. Do it before you count to three. Wayne Dyer says too, in *Manifest Your Destiny*: "Tell others how much you appreciate them." It makes most people feel good when we let them know how special they are. The problem is we often don't say it enough, or even worse, never get the chance to say it.

George Foreman in his insightful book, *George Foreman's Guide to Life* talks about "The Kiss of Death." At a funeral he says: "A kiss is how you express love and respect, not guilt and regret. That's why I call the type of kiss that comes too late ' the kiss of death.' ...If I asked around about the people weeping and wailing over the body, I'm sure I'd hear these people weren't around much when the person was alive; they always had some excuse about why they couldn't come here or there, or why it was too much trouble to do this or that. They're carrying on for themselves. Their grief is made heavier because they'll never be able to make things right...Don't wait until that person is lying in the ground. Then it's too late – way too late... And I don't just mean the physical act of hugging and kissing, I mean treating them like you love them by the way you live every day. Do as much for one another while the people you care about are still alive."

I missed some opportunities I should have taken. Reverend Foreman said he had too, including with a former spouse before she died. Perhaps you have as well. It's too late to do anything about missed opportunities, but we can make sure we're kind and attentive to those who need help now. As Benjamin Franklin commented: "Well done is better than well said."

Don't Make Assumptions

An important corollary to the rules for kindness is not to make any assumptions. My mother spent a good deal of her retirement assisting the less fortunate. She told me when she took donated food and money to the homes she visited, some of them had virtually nothing in the refrigerator, particularly at the end of the month, when people were running on empty waiting for welfare checks to come in.

The boy with a refrigerator full of food, and almost daily donuts, couldn't believe that people, within a mile or so of his middle class neighborhood, didn't have anything to eat. It's likely that there are people in the same situation within a few miles of just about anyone.

Your Unfinished Life

Killing With Kindness

It's also important not to overwhelm the receiver. Kindness should be as gracious as possible and delivered to create the least sense of self-consciousness, embarrassment and obligation. "Remember this – that there is always a proper dignity and proportion to be observed in the performance of every act of life."- Marcus Aurelius]

Giving Strength

Besides time and money, the kind man gives to his suffering fellow men of his strength, of his talents, of all his resources. He takes pains to be kind. He does not mind trouble; after emptying his purse he spends himself.

Kindliness of heart takes on all manner of trouble – faces perhaps even humiliations—to get employment for a man out of work. [There are few things somebody can do to help more than to help a job seeker find a job. It not only helps meet economic needs, but also those of self-respect. We might not always be able to help someone find a job, but we can be open to listening, making suggestions, facilitating re-training or providing support. Our employment market has undergone some permanent changes. Loss of a job can happen to almost anyone. There are relatively few people today who have real job security. This trend will only accelerate with future downsizing, outsourcing and expansion of the global economy.]

Avoiding Selfishness

Unselfishness is the first condition for the bestowing of a benefit to be a true act of kindness. The master who in ancient times looked after the health and well-being of his

On Kindness [1911] Jean Guibert

slaves, but only in order that they might work the better for him, had not the merit of charity, because he was seeking his own interest and nothing besides; in the same way, he who rendering a service to another looks upon it simply as a good investment, out of which he hopes for profit, neither acts from kindness, nor feels the joy that is brought by doing a kind act; such a one may be a good man of business, but not necessarily kind-hearted.

[In a modern example, *The Working Poor* by David Shipler mentions a farmer in the South who co-signed notes for a number of his migrant workers so they could purchase mobile homes. His well-reasoned philosophy was that it would provide him with a stable workforce if his workers had roots in the community.

Some might say he was simply looking out for himself, which in substantial part he was, but there wasn't anybody else around who was going to co-sign for these workers, and it was a benefit for them and their families. While pure kindness is most laudatory, and a less than perfect kindness may not be the purest, it can still be highly beneficial to the recipients and is better than none at all.]

The kind man is no calculator. He asks for nothing from the gift he bestows, except the joy of having helped misfortune. He has no thought of material advantage, or of praise which may accrue to him from being kind. He purposely envelops his best actions in silence and secludedness; far from himself proclaiming them from self-satisfied pride, he conceals them as carefully as others hide their faults; he wants the world to know nothing at all of his good deeds, and even the poor to benefit by them without feeling that they owe them to him.

He tries "not to let his left hand know what his right hand doeth."

Kindness Knows No Exceptions

Kindness must not only be unselfish, it must be universal. The truly kindhearted man knows no exclusion of persons in the distributing of what he has to give. He considers himself to be beholden to all sufferers.

Kindness makes no distinctions on account of nationalities, or of opinions, or of sympathies, or of antipathies; wherever it sees misery, there it speeds...The wicked even are not excluded from the solicitous tenderness of the truly kind, for as Plato remarked: "If they are forsaken by their fellow-men, they cannot help but to become more wicked." [Similarly, in *Rambam's Ladder*, Julie Salamon describes a 1906 comedy written by St. John Hankin called *The Charity That Began at Home*, in which one character expresses the sentiment: "Agreeable people don't need friends to be kind to them. They have plenty already. Disagreeable people have not."]

Kindness Must Be Discerning

Yet charity must not be practiced without discernment. On the contrary, charity should be intelligent, and far from blindly distributing the means at its disposal, should increase the value of its gifts by the opportuneness of its bestowing them. In some cases, an almsdeed means giving of money, in place of help in other forms...True kindness is fully conscious that alms are hurtful, if they unduly dispense a man from taking part in his struggle to live.

It is deplorable that the rich seem to prefer to put unquestioningly considerable sums into the hands of the

On Kindness [1911] Jean Guibert

poor, rather than to follow the needy step by step and to take the trouble to show them how to help themselves. A wise foresight, a taking into account of any probable outcome of his kind act, is essential to the kind man; and no one wishful to be kind must forget it. [Cash donations in many cases are better than no help at all. All are not suited by experience or temperament to provide personal guidance or to offer time. We all have to grow into whatever kindness skin is best for us.

My mother was a good listener and a wise counselor. When she took food, clothing or money to people, virtually all of them complete strangers before she met them, she would stay and listen to them, often for hours. I asked her once: "How can you do that all the time? I wouldn't have the patience for it." But that was her gift. And she did a lot of good doing it. But it's not something I could do well for most people. I hope writing this book might be though, just like whatever suits you best is for you. We don't have to do what someone else does, but only follow their good example in our own way.

Sometimes we get the opportunity to set an example in a completely serendipitous way. In Miami, a Brinks truck overturned dumping $500,000 in cash and 149,000 food stamps on the streets. Many people were captured on videotape picking up handfuls of bills and disappearing. A woman, who made $5.00 an hour, returned the $19.53 she got. She said: "I have children to set an example for." - Quoted from Angela Berry and *The Reader's Digest*]

Respecting Dignity

Lastly, almsgiving is the expression of true charity only when it respects the dignity and the feelings of the poor... Beware of wounding the pride of the poor: do not humble still more a man whose misery already lowers him enough in his own eyes: do not let him imagine that you are lording it over him; efface yourself for the sheer fear of offending him... It is bad enough to be tyrannized by misfortune, or by the brute forces of nature; do not crush the man who feels himself to be a failure. Do not make his chains heavier. [The beggar, the suffering, all have a place, as well as sometimes serving as a source of instruction for us. "When we treat a man as he is, we make him worse than he is. When we treat him as he already were what he could potentially be, we make him what he should be."- Goethe

A late attorney friend of mine, who was a great model of kindness and character, used to take walks early in the morning, sometimes leaving a fifty-dollar bill between the front doors of people who needed it. He once met a total stranger, whose brother was being held in the county jail for a minor offense, which required the payment of several hundred dollars in bail. He reached into his pocket and gave the man the money to have his brother released. He died suddenly in his sleep in his mid-fifties of a heart attack on an Easter Sunday morning. He left behind him a great number of clients he never billed at all, or who were billed only a portion of what they owed him. But that wasn't what mattered most. His kindness to others, including me, was legendary. Both he and his loving wife served as consistent models of extraordinary caring in a variety of ways. She still continues to do so using her own special gifts to assist those in need.]

It may be that the respect you show will not always be appreciated by the poor, but it is certain that the charity which is overbearing always irritates and at the same time depresses them...the greatest benefactors of the poor are assuredly those who strive to hide their own better fortune, and to bridge over the distance between the poor and themselves. By showing itself retiring, almost shy, their generosity clothes itself with the winning charm of true kindliness.

True Kindness Is Gracious

St. Paul said: "God loveth the cheerful giver." The pleasant smile with which kindheartedness enhances the good deeds is called graciousness. It is graciousness which makes our almsdeeds look natural, unaffected and pleasing. For surely the poverty which you relieve [and not always monetary], calls for your tact in dealing with it quite as much as for your alms; the needy rejoice as much for rejoicing of heart, as much as they do for bread, and all food nourishes the better for being, so to speak, steeped in joy... it is equally our vocation to heal the wounds of the soul, by uttering kind and gracious words. Graciousness then is like a finishing touch given to the beauty of charity.

It is very sure that the tongue soon becomes the ready servant of a kind mind. Sympathetic words have for the listener's soul a healing and nourishing virtue which calms suffering. The kind man takes heed lest he wound by oversharply criticizing or by indulging in witticisms, clever though they may be, but galling beyond belief for him who is their butt. He does not make fun of his neighbor; but on the contrary knows very well how, tactfully and without flattering, to praise where praise is deserved. He is careful never in conversing with another to recall any painful memory, but instinctively and quite unaffectedly talks, and makes others talk, of things pleasant, wholesome and in some way or other uplifting.

[Another exemplary man, who serves as a model of character for many, wrote out a biblical quotation for me many years ago as an encouragement for me to improve my frequently coarse language. Conveniently, it also serves as an excellent guide to spoken kindness: "Let no foul speech whatever come out of your mouth, but only what serves well to improve the occasion, so as to add a blessing to the listener" - *The Bible.*]

Kindheartedness Dares Everything

Watch the daily dealings of a man who is thoroughly good-hearted. He is affable to all who come across him; he never lets people suspect that he is tired of them and of their talk...He does not think at all about his own pleasures or even interests; his thoughts refuse to be self-centered; all his preoccupation and all his solicitude is for the well being of others. His watchful considerateness gives him marvelous intuition; he feels instinctively what will displease, and avoids it; he recognizes on the instant what will please, and does it...His kindheartedness has come to be far more than a mere good-natured wish to help; it dares everything.

Nothing so surely takes away one's peace of mind as knowing oneself to be little thought of. Of all human sufferings, humiliation is the most keenly felt. Scorn, whether betrayed by manner, put into humbling words, or manifested by contemptuous treatment, is fatal where it wounds, save for him who has learned...to care not at all for the judgments of men, and to be content with the good testimony rendered him by God and his own conscience.

But few of us have grown to this. We feel as the rest of men. Like them we cannot help caring. When humbled we are inevitably cast down. Kind words, and a show of respect and sympathy, are the medicine we want in our trouble. Put us where we can feel we are understood and thought well of, and forthwith we get our spirits back and are well again. There is no occasion to be sparing of kind words that spell peace to our fellow-men. Cheerfulness is the outcome of peace of heart.

True Kindness Is Loving

Kindness is more than gracious. It is loving. A kind heart loves those to whom it does good and the love it bestows is above every other of its gifts. Kindness may begin in mere pity with words of sympathy, but the more it grows the more it leads to the doing of kind and generous actions, to the bestowing on the needy at the cost of self-denial. [The kinder we are, the kinder we will become. We will grow not just to give from our excess, but from our substance: "He who gathered much had no excess and he who gathered little had no lack." – *The Bible*.

William of Occam [1288-1348], an English Franciscan friar and philosopher, looked upon it also as a matter of humility: "It is vain to do with more, what can be done with less."

Rambam's Ladder discusses Maimonides' "Ladder of Giving." Maimonides was a famous Jewish rabbi and philosopher.

Julie Salamon describes the Hebrew word *tzedakah*, which is thought to mean charity, derived from the Hebrew word "tzedek", or justice. Both Jewish and Christian traditions, and others, arrive at the same conclusion, that kindness is a matter of justice, not simply an option. The justice of kindness doesn't just relate to money, but to food, expertise or whatever else someone can offer.]

Lacordaire said: "God has willed that no good should be done to a man unless the gift be sanctified by love; and that heartlessness should be forever incapable either of imparting light or of inspiring virtue." [To give without the proper attitude is an attitude that requires improvement for the higher benefit of both giver and recipient, but even when love is absent, some help is provided. The purity of kindness is to be aspired to, but less than perfect kindness is a start.]

"The more we are urged to feel affectionate, the more we draw back, for to do other than freely, is unnatural to man." [We should just grow at our own rate. Forced kindness isn't the stuff that changes minds and hearts.]

"If to be loved is good, to love is better. A faithful friend is a strong defense and he that hath found him hath found treasure."

The Way To Become Kind

The Sort Of Mind A Man Has Leads To His Being Kind-Hearted Or Otherwise

There is a kind mind as there is a kind heart. Kind thoughts, kind words and kind deeds are, in general, naturally inseparable and dependent each one on the others. For it is the mind that shows the heart where, and how, and why to be kind. It is the mind that frees the heart from the groundless fears and foolish suspicions that act as a drag upon its kindly impulses; while in return, the heart softens the mind and makes it kind.

To understand a man is to afford him an immense satisfaction. The moment he is understood he begins to feel comforted. It is just because he longs to be understood that it is a relief for him to tell his troubles. Once understood, he has a weight off his mind.

[Have you ever had the experience of listening to someone who's troubled, perhaps offering a few suggestions as you listen, but for the most part just listening? After people have shared troubling thoughts, it's not uncommon for them to say something such as: "Thanks. You helped me a lot." Our response is likely to be: "I didn't do anything. All I did was listen." But the value comes from letting someone put the troublesome thoughts they have rumbling around inside their head out in front of them by expressing them to someone else. By doing so, they sometimes gain perspectives and insights they may never have had otherwise. Being a good listener can be a valuable kindness.]

Even the most fervent of believers likes to feel that, besides God, there is some being who takes notice of him, who understands him, who cares for him, and who values him for whatever steadiness of good purpose his apparent fickleness conceals, for whatever degree of virtue has survived the weaknesses which his many failures witness against him, for whatever little moral strength he displays when beaten down by misfortunes. Now that someone should show himself intelligently kind and intelligently sympathetic—a form of goodwill possible only where thought is deep and sure—is just what those who have gone under, whether it be through deplorable stupidity of their own, or through cruel misunderstanding on the part of other people, are longing for.

It is a mistake to look upon kindheartedness as giving no more than a gracious cram [addition] to character; it is a real source of intellectual light. For kindness develops in a man a new sense which in delicacy is second to none. The blind man perceives by touch what his eyes cannot see; and a thousand things in life which escape the mind, the heart knows by its own intuition. Pascal has put a great truth into the well-known words: "The heart has reasons that reason cannot understand." [Blaise Pascal (1623-1662) was a renowned French mathematician and philosopher. His most famous philosophical work, *Pensées*, is a collection of personal thoughts on human suffering and faith in God. It contains the renowned "Pascal's wager" which claims to prove that belief in God is rational with the following argument: "If God does not exist, one will lose nothing by believing in him, while if he does exist, one will lose everything by not believing."]

The heart can communicate to the intellect, elements of knowledge which of itself the intellect was powerless to acquire. [It can take a long time for us to reach that point. As a speaker said in a lecture I heard: "The distance from the head to the heart is only about twelve inches, but it can take us forty or fifty years to learn how to have your heart touch your head."]

How A Man Cannot Be Truly Kind, Unless He Has The Will To Be So

It is very true that not all kindnesses are equally deliberate; some people have naturally gentle and sympathetic natures

On Kindness [1911] Jean Guibert

– to be kind they need only follow their own bent. Other characters, sterner or colder [or more self absorbed and self centered] have almost to force themselves to be kind; they are like the seeds which must be ground in a mill [of life experience and personal growth] before they yield the oil they contain.

Nevertheless, even the naturally kindhearted, those on whom has fallen "the great good fortune to be born good" [or those who have grown to be] should bear in mind that no act of virtue is easy to put into practice, and that kindnesses are all the more welcome for being premeditated and carried out under difficulties.

The noblest of souls have had to struggle before they could be rid of an instinctive tendency to be harsh and ungracious. St. Francis de Sales avows that to make himself kind and gentle he had to work long and hard. [St Francis de Sales was the Bishop of Geneva, Switzerland by age 35. A friend of St. Vincent de Paul, he was a prolific writer.]

St. Vincent de Paul says it was a wearisome fight. "I turned to God and I asked him earnestly to change my hard and repelling temper, and to give me in its place a meek and gentle spirit, and by the grace of Our Lord, and with a little attention which I myself gave to keep natural impulses under control, I have at least partially got rid of the surly temper with which I was born." [More likely developed, as we develop some of our other baser characteristics.]

Once kindness becomes active, it is sure to become generous. If it is slow in getting to work, it is for the will to insist, to spur it on. When we cannot give from enthusiasm, let us at least give from sheer logic. A spontaneous gift, the effect of an impulse, is often more gracious, but a gift, the giving of which has been carefully pondered and perhaps reluctantly resolved upon, is equally meritorious. [Some kindness decisions might also benefit from reflection and can properly keep us from extending kindnesses that might not be helpful.]

True Kindliness Is A Quality Of The Heart

We must begin by studying ourselves, in order to know our faults and our resources. We must have an ideal befitting us individually to look up to, for the plan of life varies from man to man according to his aptitudes and circumstances. We must set bravely to work, and by uninterrupted efforts repress our instincts for evil, and develop our tendencies for good. [There can be further benefit. As English writer and social critic John Ruskin noted: "Every duty we omit obscures some truth we should have known."]

Conclusion

If you are convinced of the truth of what you have read in this little book about kindness, make a firm resolution henceforth never to pour one single drop of gall into anyone's cup, no matter whose it may be, and never to suffer a single day to pass without having shed a ray of happiness on some poor, troubled soul.

> "Kindness is more a function of
> the heart than the wallet."
> - Wayne Dyer

> "Your way of giving is much more important
> than what you give"
> - Vietnamese proverb

Chapter 3

Kindness *[1892]*

Frederick W. Faber

[What follows is a summary of *Kindness* by Frederick Faber, with commentary. It contains marvelous insights conveyed with unusual clarity, often accompanied by a literary and lyrical quality, which those who admire good writing will appreciate.]

Man is no doubt very weak. He can only be passive in a thunderstorm or run in an earthquake. The odds are against him when he is managing his ship in a hurricane or when pestilence is raging in the house where he lives. Heat and cold, drought and rain are his masters. He is weaker than an elephant, and subordinate to the east wind. This is all very true. Nevertheless man has considerable powers, considerable enough to leave him, as proprietor of this planet, in possession of at least as much comfortable jurisdiction as most landed proprietors have in a free country. He has one power in particular, which is not sufficiently dwelt on, and with which we will at present occupy ourselves. It is the power of making the world happy, or at least of so greatly diminishing the amount of unhappiness in it, as to make it a quite different world than it is at present. This power is called kindness.

The worst kinds of unhappiness, as well as the greatest amount of it, come from our conduct to each other. If our conduct therefore were under the control of kindness, it would be nearly the opposite of what it is, and so the state of the world would be almost reversed.

Kindness is the overflowing of self upon others. We put others in the place of self. We treat them as we should wish to be treated ourselves. Kindness is the coming to the rescue of others when they need it, when it is in our power to supply what they need.

Let us consider the office of kindness in the world in order that we may get a clearer idea of it. It makes life more endurable...There are many men to whom life is always approaching the unbearable. It stops just short of it.

It is true that we make ourselves more unhappy than other people make us. [More often than not, it is our thoughts that do us in, rather than the objective circumstances. As Joel Osteen remarks: "Our thoughts affect our emotions. We feel exactly the way we think...Your circumstances don't have you down. Your thoughts about your circumstances have you down...Make a choice to keep your mind focused on the higher things...Fortunately, we can dig a new river, one going in a positive direction. The way we do so is one thought at a time." – [*Your Best Life Now: 7 Steps To Living At Your Full Potential"*]

Kindness [1892] Frederick W. Faber

Kindness Aids Those Failing In Purpose

There are some men whose practical talents are completely swamped by the keenness of their sense of injustice. They go through life as failures, because of the pressure of injustice upon themselves, or the sight of its pressing upon others has unmanned them ...They had much in them; but they have died without anything having come from them. [Perhaps more realistically, not as much as they would have hoped for.] Kindness steps forward to remedy this evil. Each solitary kind action that is done, the whole world over, is working briskly in its own sphere to restore the balance between right and wrong to correct itself and remain in equilibrium...Kindness allies itself with the right, to invade the wrong and to beat it off the earth.

Gods To Each Other

Kindness has converted more sinners than zeal, eloquence or learning; and these last three have never converted anyone, unless they were kind also. In short, kindness makes us Gods to each other. [A feeling many of us can identify with when we have been distressed, or have faced a critical turning point in our lives, and someone has been there for us.]

Kindness, Character and Undeveloped Nobility

What does kindness do for those to whom we show it? The great consequence, is the immense power of kindness in bringing out the good points of the character of others. Almost all men have more good in them than the ordinary intercourse of the world enables us to discover. Most men, from glimpses we now and then obtain, carry with them to the grave much undeveloped nobility.

Life is seldom so varied or so adventurous as to enable a man to unfold all that is in him. But we can try to liberate all the potential for kindness that resides inside us. [It's an energizing thought to know that we have so much inside us to give, waiting to be developed, if we can only use the key of kindness to help us become what we're capable of becoming. As Samuel Smiles said in his classic 1859 book *Self Help*: "Character is power, more than knowledge is power."]

Kindness Reveals The Man

[Most of us pass churches in our travels, frequently noticing the often cleverly worded topics for the upcoming sermon as an inducement to attend. At a church on the corner of Eighty-sixth and West End in New York City, the sign read: "The Power of Knowing Who You Are." If we know who we are, we'll be kinder. If we're kinder, we'll get to know ourselves better and a lot sooner. Becoming kinder is a matter of growth that leads to increased and genuine happiness. For some it may never take place. "Quit your childhood, my friend, and wake up", as French philosopher Jean-Jacques Rousseau said. Selfishness and lack of consideration for others is a childish habit that child-adults don't outgrow. "It is amazing how much emotion a little mental concept like 'my' can generate." -*The New* Earth - Eckhart Tolle.]

Kindness leads the way into true adulthood, self-recognition, emotional maturity and happiness. Kindness not only reveals itself to external spectators. It reveals a man to himself. It rouses long dormant self-respect.

Kindness [1892] Frederick W. Faber

Kind Acts Impact The World

I can look out over the earth at any hour, and I see, in spirit, innumerable angels threading the crowds of men, and hindering evil by all manner of artifices which shall not interfere with the freedom of a man's will. They are flitting everywhere, making gloomy men smile, and angry men grow meek, and sick men cease to groan, lighting up hope in the eyes of the dying, sweetening the heart of the bitter, and adroitly turning men away from evil just when they seem on the verge of committing it. They seem to have strange power. Men listen to them who have been deaf to the pleading of angels. They gain admittance into hearts before the doors of which grace has lost its patience and gone away. No sooner are the doors open than these veiled messengers, these cunning ministers of God, have gone and returned with lightning-like speed and brought grace back with them. They are the most versatile in their operations. One while they are the spies of grace, another while they bear the brunt of the battle, and for more than five thousand years they hardly have known the meaning of defeat. These are daily acts of kindness from the rising to the setting of the sun. ...If we have no notion of the far-reaching mischief that unkindness does, so neither can we rightly estimate the good which kindness may do. [Such magnificent power - available to each and every one of us.]

Kindness Makes Men Kinder and Propagates Itself

Kindness is the most gracious attitude one man can assume toward another. Kindness is infectious. No kind action ever stopped with itself. One kind action leads to another. By one, we commit ourselves to more than one.

This is the greatest work that kindness does to others – that it makes them kind themselves.

Perhaps an act of kindness never dies, but extends to the invisible undulations of its influence over the breadth of centuries. Thus there is no better thing which we can do for others than to be kind to them...["Try to do a beautiful impossibility and you'll never be a failure." – Mother Teresa]

Blessings of Kindness

Let us see how kindness blesses us. Foremost among the ways are how it helps us to get clear of selfishness. It also tends to rapidly set in as a well formed habit.

Selfishness is in no slight degree a way we regard things. Kindness alters our view by altering our point of view. Does anything more effectually affect our spiritual growth?

Selfishness indeed furnishes us with a grand opportunity - the opportunity to hate ourselves because of the odiousness of this self-worship. But how few of us have either the depth or the bravery to profit by this magnificent occasion. On the whole, selfishness must be put down or our progress will cease. Perhaps we may never come to be quite unselfish. However, there is but one road toward that which is kindness; every step taken on that road is a long stride heavenward [and/or to our betterment and decency as human beings]. Inward happiness almost always follows a kind action.

Kindness and Humility

Kindness almost always assures the exercise of humility. A proud man is seldom a kind man. Humility makes us kind, and kindness makes us humble. It would be foolish to say that humility is an easy virtue. The very lowest degree of it is a difficult height to climb. But this much may be said for kindness, that it is the easiest road to humility.

While kindness lifts us so high, it sweetly keeps us low. [As Mother Teresa counseled: "If you are humble, nothing will touch you, neither praise, nor disgrace, because you know who you are." - and we gain all the resultant benefit of personal growth that comes with that.

The only real wisdom is humility. Carlos Castenada warned that we should stop trying to uphold our own importance. Instead, we should focus on the words of Benjamin Franklin: "A man wrapped up in himself makes a very small bundle."]

St. Vincent de Paul confirms this by saying: "Humility and charity are the two master chords: one, the lowest; the other, the highest; all the others are dependent on them. Therefore, it is necessary above all to maintain ourselves in these two virtues; for observe well that the preservation of the whole edifice depends on the foundation and the roof."

Michael Gellert strikes a similar chord in *The Way of The Small*: "Unlike other creatures, we are unusually preoccupied with our self-importance...However, if we could only see that our smallness is what makes us great, perhaps we wouldn't need to pretend to be great by our inflation or grandiosity... We should exercise modesty, self-restraint and reliance on inner worth rather than external brilliance."]

Benefits of Kindness

Kindness does so much for us: it watches the thoughts, controls the words, and helps us to unlearn man's inveterate habit of criticism. It makes us thoughtful and considerate. Detached acts of kindness may be an offspring of impulse [such as dropping money into the Salvation's Army's Red Kettle at holiday time]. Yet he is mostly a good man whose impulses are good. [One wouldn't have been likely to put something in the kettle, if he/she didn't have some caring instincts to begin with.]

But in the long run, habitual kindness is not a mere series of generous impulses, but steadfast growth of generous deliberation. Much thought must go to consistent kindness. And much self-denying legislation.

A kind man is a man who is never self-occupied. [That's a tall order. Being able to do it even most of the time would be very admirable.]

Kind Thoughts

Governing Our Thoughts

The thoughts of men are a world by themselves, vast and populous. Each man's thoughts are a world to himself. There is an astonishing breadth of thoughts of even the most narrow-minded man. Thus we all have an interior world to govern and we are really the only ones who govern it effectually. Our character is formed within. It is manufactured in the world of our thoughts, and there we must go to influence it. He, who is master there, is master everywhere. He has himself completely under control, if he has learned to control his thoughts. ["A person is what he thinks about all day long." – Ralph Waldo Emerson

Kindness [1892] Frederick W. Faber

"The thought manifests as the word
The word manifests as the deed
The deed develops into habit
And the habit hardens into character.
So watch with thought and its ways with care
And let it spring from love
Born out of concern for all beings"
- The Buddha - Quoted from *The Practice of Kindness*, Conari Press]

Privacy Of Thoughts

The power of suffering is the grandest merchandise of life, and it is also manufactured in the world of thought. It seems to me that our thoughts are a more true measure of ourselves than our actions are. They are not under the control of human respect. It is not easy for them to be ashamed of themselves. They have no witnesses ... They are not bound to keep within certain limits or to observe certain proprieties. The struggle which so often ensues within us before we can bring ourselves to do our duty goes on entirely within our thoughts. It is our secret, and men cannot put us to shame because of it.

Thoughts Show True Character

As an impulse will sometimes show more of our real character than what we do after deliberation, our first thoughts will often reveal to us faults of disposition which outward restraints will keep from issuing in action. Actions have their external hindrances, while our thoughts better disclose our possibilities of good or evil. Of course, there is a most true sense in which the conscientious effort to cure a fault is a better indication of our character, than the fault we have not succeeded in curing.

Kind Thoughts Are Consequential

If our thoughts be of this importance, and also if kindness be of this importance, it follows that kind thoughts must be of immense consequence. If a man habitually has kind thoughts of others, he is not far from being a saint. All his thoughts are kind and he does not checker them with unkindly ones. Even when sudden passions or angry excitements have thrown them into commotion, they settle down into a kindly humor and cannot settle otherwise. These men are rare. Kind thoughts are rarer than either kind words or kind deeds. They imply a great deal of thinking about others. This is itself rare. But they imply also a great deal of thinking about others without the thoughts being criticisms. This is rarer still.

Judging Others

Active minded men are naturally most given to criticism. Such men must make kind thoughts a defense against self. By sweetening the fountain of their thoughts, they will destroy the bitterness of their judgment.

[Kind thoughts defend us against ourselves and against being judgmental of others. In spite of what we might think, we often lack enough information to judge the actions of others. It is common for people to think that they know it all, or most of it, when they only typically operate with bits of information. As Thoreau succinctly remarked, we often "count some parts and say I know."

If we are judging others, there is something wrong with

our thought process. As Mother Teresa said: "If you love people, you have no time to judge them."]

The kind-thoughted man has no rights to defend, no self-importance to push. He thinks moderately of himself, and with so much honesty, that he thinks thus of himself with tranquility. Others find him so pleasant to deal with that love follows him wherever he goes. [Many of us probably know a few people who are loved by all. When we look to their characteristics, we will probably find many of those mentioned here.]

Kind Interpretations

There is one class of kind thoughts which must be dwelt upon apart. I allude to kind interpretations. The habit of not judging others is one which is very difficult to acquire, and which is generally not acquired till very late in the spiritual life.

Men's actions are very difficult to judge. Their real character depends in a great measure on the motives which prompt them, and those motives are invisible to us. Appearances are often against what we afterward discover to have been deeds of virtue. Nobody can judge men but God, and we can hardly obtain a higher or more reverent view of God than that which represents him to us as judging men with perfect knowledge, unperplexed certainty and undisturbed compassion.

[It can be a good test to consider these three factors when judging others. Some people seem to have no trouble with the unperplexed certainty part, so frequently being convinced of the absolute correctness of their own judgments, as erroneous as they might be. In *Living Faith*,

Jimmy Carter tells about Miriam "Ma" Ferguson, who was elected Governor of Texas in 1924. There was a debate about whether Spanish was to be permitted in schools. She was opposed to it. She concluded her argument by holding up a Bible and saying: "If English was good enough for Jesus Christ, it's good enough for Texans!" Being grandly self-assured of one's opinions does nothing to ensure their correctness.

Sensible people realize they lack perfect knowledge, particularly of another's motives and actions, and recognize that their level of compassion may also leave something to be desired. Nevertheless, many judge others at least occasionally, sometimes regularly.

"When you judge another person, you do not define them. You define yourself as someone who needs to judge others...Stop judging. Just be an observer. You don't have enough information to judge anyone else...Point out what you like about someone, rather than what they're doing wrong...Celebrate the finest qualities of others." - (*10 Secrets For Success and Inner Peace* - Wayne Dyer)

It can also be safer not to be so sure of what we are capable of doing and not doing, even if we consider ourselves to be "a righteous person", as I mistakenly have done in the past. Someone being judged needs more kindness than judgment.]

The habit of judging is so nearly incurable, and its cure is such an almost interminable process, that we must concentrate ourselves for a long while on keeping it in check. This check is found in kind interpretations. [Giving someone else the benefit of the doubts, even if we can't envision them all, or even if we don't agree with what someone else has done.] Have we not always found in our experiences that on the whole our kind interpretations are truer than our harsh ones? What mistakes we have made in judging others! We should depress our own ideas more and elevate our generous belief in others.

[A priest lecturing at Malvern, a well known retreat center outside Philadelphia, mentioned that he had attended a meeting conducted by an attorney who didn't stand up when he was introduced to him, a courtesy frequently extended to clergymen. He also said the man wasn't too cordial either. He quickly judged him not to be a nice person. Later, he found out that the man had bone cancer, had a few months to live and was incapable of standing. It spoke highly to me that the speaker was willing to efface himself to provide us with a worthwhile lesson. Sometimes it's better to reserve judgment. Initial ones are often far off the mark. They might also be clearly different if we could see "the big picture"– which many times we can't.]

Consequences of Being Judgmental

A man is very much himself what he thinks of others. A man who was of a higher eminence before will soon, by his harsh judgments of others, sink to the level of his own judgments. When you hear a man attribute meanness to another, you may be sure not only that the critic is an ill-natured man, but that he has got a similar element of meanness in himself, or is fast sinking to it. A man is always capable himself of a sin, which he thinks another is capable of, or which he himself is capable of imputing to another. ["He who stands upright should be watchful, lest he fall." - *The Bible*]

Even a well-founded suspicion more or less degrades a man. His suspicion may be verified, and he may escape some material harm by having cherished the suspicion, but he is unavoidably the worse man in consequence for having entertained it. ["It is more useful to be aware of a single weakness in oneself, than to be aware of a thousand weaknesses in someone else." - The Dalai Lama]

Thoughts Govern The Tongue

The practice of kind thoughts is our main help to that complete government of the tongue, which we all so much covet.

The interior of the soul, through habitual kindness of thought, is greater than our words can tell. To such a man life is a perpetual bright evening, with all things calm and fragrant and restful. ["Your life is what your thoughts make it." – Marcus Aurelius]

Kind Words

Kind Words Make Others Happy

Kind words are the music of the world. A kind word – perhaps a mere report of a kind word – has been enough to set all things straight and has been the commencement of enduring friendships. [There is something about the quality of kind words said about us, that seems to even surpass kind words said to us, perhaps because we know we've been raised in the eyes of others, not just our own.]

Words have a power of their own for good and evil, which I believe to be more influential and energetic over our fellow men than even actions. It is by voice and by

Kindness [1892] Frederick W. Faber

words that men mesmerize each other. Oh, it would be worth going through fire and water to find the opportunity of saying fine words! The occasions for saying them do not lie scattered over life at great distances from each other. They occur continually.

The habit of saying kind words is quickly formed, and when once formed, it is not speedily lost. I have often thought that unkindness is very much of a mental habit. I believe cruelty to be less uncommon than real inward unkindness. [Is there anybody alive who hasn't thought, "Oh, if only he/she knew what I was thinking right now!"]

Not only is kindness due to everyone, but a special kindness is due to everyone. Kindness is not kindness, unless it is special.

Kind Words Make Us Happy

The double reward of kind words is the happiness they cause in others and the happiness they cause in ourselves. The very process of uttering them is a happiness in itself. Is there any happiness in the world like the happiness of a disposition made happy by the happiness of others? There is no joy to be compared with it.

Kind words make us happy in ourselves. They produce in us a sense of quiet restfulness, like that which accompanies the consciousness of being forgiven when we have done wrong. We become kinder by saying kind words and this itself is a further reward. Every thing that makes us gentle has at the same time a tendency to make us contrite.

Your Unfinished Life

Kindness and Truthfulness

Kind words make us truthful. Oh, this is what we want, to be true! It is our insincerity, our manifold inseparable falseness, which is the load under which we groan. There is no slavery but untruthfulness.

Kind Words Can Be Brief

[It doesn't take many kind words to be effective. As Mother Teresa said: "Kind words can be short and easy to speak, but their echoes are truly endless." Mother Teresa was often brief, sometimes to the point of terseness, yet remains a shining example of what kindness is all about. Even if you're "not a talker", saying the right kind words, even few but well chosen ones, can make a real difference, particularly when combined with deeds: "Say little and do much."-Quoted from *Rambam's Ladder*. Shammai was a noted Jewish rabbi and scholar.]

Kindness and Cleverness

In some respects, a clever man is more likely to be kind than a man who is not clever, because his mind is wider, and takes in a broader range, and is capable of looking at things from different points of view. But there are other respects in which it is harder for a clever man to be kind, especially in his words. He has a temptation – and it is one of those temptations which appear sometimes to border of the irresistible, to say clever things, and somehow clever things are hardly ever kind things. He is forever jostling charity by the pungency of his criticisms, and wounding justice by the revelation of secrets. [Il n'est pas ordinaire, que celui qui fait rire se fasse estimer. - La Bruyere. Loosely translated, this French phrase means: It is not typical that the one who makes people laugh, makes himself valued. Jean de La Bruyere (1645-1696) was a French moralist.]

Kind Listening

There is also a grace of kind listening, as well as the grace of kind speaking. Some men listen with an abstracted air, which shows that their thoughts are elsewhere. Or they seem to listen, but by wide answers and irrelevant questions, show that they have been occupied with their own thoughts, as being more interesting, at least in their own estimation, than what you have been saying.

Some hear you to the end, then forthwith begin to talk to you about a similar experience which has befallen them, making your case an illustration of their own.

Kind listening is often an act of the most delicate interior mortification and is a great assistance to kind speaking. [Kind listening is a gracious art. When others are telling us something that goes on to the point that it can make our eyes glaze over, it is the exceptional person who can focus on the needs of others. A collateral kindness is to be a considerate speaker, trying to recognize when we have perhaps gone on too long. I've been the source of making some eyes glaze over also. I'm working on it!]

Proper Manner For Kindness

The unselfishness of speedily and gracefully distracting ourselves from self is singularly difficult to practise. It is weary work cleaning old bricks to build a new house with. The more humble we are, the more kindly we shall talk; the more kindly we talk, the more humble we shall grow.

An air of superiority is foreign to the genius of kindness. The look of kindness is that of one receiving a favor, rather than conferring it. Experience true joy, not just the mere happiness we get when receiving something ourselves.

Weak and full of wants as we are ourselves, we must make up our minds, or rather take heart, to do some good to this poor world while we are in it. Kind words are our chief implement for this work. [Kind words are highly efficient and easily tendered. Some may feel that they don't have the focus or the time for kind actions, but anyone can offer a few appropriate and sincere kind words.]

Kind Actions

Kindness Received and Returned

Let us think today that there are multitudes in heaven who are there because of kind actions: many are there for doing them, many for having them done to them...If we look back over the past twenty or thirty years, it is amazing to consider the number of kind actions which have been done to us. They are almost beyond our counting. Indeed, we feel that those we remember are hardly so numerous as those we have forgotten, not because of ingratitude, but because of the distractions of life and the shortness of memory.

[What's the kindest thing anyone has ever done for you? If you can't think of it right away, it just underscores the point that many of us can forget. I couldn't remember either - and not because there weren't many occasions. Debts owed to spouses, partners, parents, grandparents, brothers and sisters, children, grandchildren, aunts, uncles, cousins, friends, teachers, coaches, counselors, rabbis, ministers, priests, nuns, co-workers, authors we've read, strangers we have met who have given us directions or helped us when our cars broke down, or who gave us fair treatment or money.

In her very interesting book, *The Right Words At The Right Time*, Marlo Thomas asked celebrities what made critical turning points in their lives. Former NBC News anchor Tom Brokaw related how a college professor got his attention by telling him that he should drop out of college because he wasn't applying himself. After dropping out for a while, he realized how his being less than serious was screwing up his life. He later returned to college with dedication to purpose and began his road to success.

Actress Sarah Jessica Parker, whose family had limited resources, tells how a dance instructor made it possible for her to attend dancing classes on a scholarship and how she was able to continue her study in New York as a result of her instructor's efforts, leading ultimately to her success as a television and movie star. While your efforts might not put someone on the road to fame, they can help people at critical times and make similarly dramatic improvements in their lives.]

We're not only the sum total of all of our own actions, but of those who have taken their time to help us. The thought of all of them melts our hearts. ...We seem to have stood all our lives under the constant dripping of beneficent showers. Let us think also how little we have deserved all these kind actions, not only as far as God is concerned, but also as far as our fellow creatures are concerned. There is no one who has not received tenfold more kindness himself than he has shown to others.

Kindness To The Rescue

From how many evils have such people not also rescued us! We know of many; but there are many more of which we do not know. We can hardly tell what we should have been had we been treated one whit less kindly than we have been. It is frightening to think what we should have been had people been less kind to us.

Kindness Is Not Difficult

Hardly out of twenty kind actions does one call for anything like an effort of self-denial on our part. Easiness is the rule and difficulty the exception.

[George Foreman in his wise book *George Foreman's Guide to Life* shows that even as easy as a small kindness can be, some people won't even do that, not because they don't notice the need, but just because they don't want to, even when the need is placed squarely in front of them: "It reminded me of the day my Mom sent me to a little corner store right across the street from our house. I didn't have anything to wear to school, so I had to stay home. Mom had given me a note for the lady who owned the store. I couldn't read yet, so Mom said to me, "Take this letter to the store and give it to the lady, and wait for her answer. The store owner handed me back the note, and told me to tell my Mom, 'We don't have any'. So I went home with that message. 'You mean she didn't have any collard greens?' my mother asked. I said, 'Oh yes she did. I saw them right in front of the counter.' How I wished at that moment that I could read and have spared my Mom some heartache and embarrassment. She started to cry and told me, 'All I asked her was to let me have two bunches of greens to feed my children and that I

would give her twenty-five cents at the end of the week.' "
What seems insignificant to many, at the right time can be a large help indeed – and so often, so easy to do.

Little Things Mean A Lot

The song *Little Things Mean A Lot*, sung by Kitty Kallen and written by Edith Lindeman and Carl Stutz, helped make this a memorable phrase in the nineteen fifties. The thought rings so true because most of us know it from our own experience:

"Give me your hand when I've lost my way
Give me your shoulder to cry on
Whether the day is bright or gray
Give me your heart to rely on…
Little things mean a lot."

Many want to do the big things, but not as many want to do the little things. Mother Teresa had much to say about little things:

- "Little things are indeed little, but being faithful in little things is a great thing."
- "We can do no great things, only small things with great love."
- "Be faithful in small things, because it is in them that your strength lies."
- "There should be less talk; a preaching point is not a meeting point. What do you do then? Take a broom and clean someone's house. That says enough."

- "It is not how much we do, but how much love we put in the doing. It's not how much we give, but how much love we put in the giving."

Some might say: "How can I help? I don't have much myself." Perhaps, but probably far more than Mother Teresa and her sister nuns had. We always have enough to help someone in some way. As she said of herself and her sisters: "We, the unwilling, led by the unknowing, are doing the impossible for the ungrateful. We have done so much, for so long, with so little, we are now qualified to do anything with nothing."

Making A Difference

My mother told me a little story a few months before she died, which I've seen several times since. I retold it in her eulogy because it was so much like her: A man walking along a beach noticed that the tide had stranded hundreds of starfish so that they couldn't be taken back out to sea by the tide. He saw a young boy picking them up one by one and throwing them back into the ocean. The man said to him impatiently, "What possible difference can you hope to make? There are thousands of these things stranded up here. The boy picked up another one, tossed it into the water, then looked at the man and said: "It makes a difference to this one."

We might not stop to think of it often, but little things done for someone, particularly at a critical time, can make all the difference. My father went to Eckels School of Mortuary Science in Philadelphia in the 1930's. His mortuary school tuition was about $150 a semester, which was a substantial sum at the time. My father was frugal, but he was only able to save part of the tuition. After he completed the first half of the year, he went to Mr. Eckels and said that he wouldn't be able to return because he didn't have the money. The owner told him that he was a good student and to come back to school and to repay the money when he could. My father always spoke appreciatively of the kindness Mr. Eckels showed him. Without it, he may never had been able to become a funeral director. Little things at the right time can be very big things.

Many people need a break to help them get over some rough spots, like a single mom whose car needs to be repaired so she can get to work or someone who needs part time work to help them make ends meet. You can be the critical force that helps someone get over the hump. You'll know when it's time. Like the man on the rainy night mentioned at the beginning of the book, it will be brought to your attention.

Many self-help books emphasize the principle that the secret of happiness isn't in getting service, it's in giving it. Perhaps some might not have the patience to work with handicapped children or to help someone learn how to read, but those people might not have the money, time, construction, mechanical, technical, accounting, teaching, legal or medical talent you have either. Whatever kind of work you do, or whatever disposition you have, you can use it in some way to help others. "Each of us has his or her own path of service. Dedicate yourself to the call of your heart and see where it leads you." - Quoted from *The Practice of Kindness*, Conari Press]

Kindness Is Economical And Expects Nothing

When kindness does call for an effort, how noble and self-rewarding is the sacrifice! We always gain more than we lose. There is something very economical about the generosity of kindness. A little goes a long way.

Kindness Can Just Be Fairness

[Kindness doesn't always involve giving someone anything extra. It's simply a kindness not to take anything away unjustly. Malcolm Gladwell in his engrossing best seller *Blink* provided interesting insight into the orchestra audition process.

Screens are often used today in auditions, so that there will be no sexual or appearance bias toward the aspiring musicians and "so the judges can listen, not with their eyes, but with their ears and their hearts."...In the last thirty years, since screens became commonplace, the number of women in the top U.S. orchestras has increased fivefold.

"The very first time the new rules for auditions were used, we were looking for new violinists, remembers Herb Weksleblatt, a tuba player for the Metropolitan Opera in New York, who led the fight for blind auditions at the Met in the mid-1960's. 'All the winners were women. That would simply have never happened before. Up until that point, we had maybe three women in the whole orchestra. I remember that after it was announced that the four women had won, one guy was absolutely furious at me.' He said: 'You're going to be remembered as the SOB who brought women into this orchestra.' " How many fine female musicians were denied the rightful opportunity they could have had to play in that orchestra, and many other orchestras, in all the years before that, because of lack of basic fairness? Just simple fairness can be a great kindness.]

Effects of Kindness

The amount of kindness bears no proportion to the effect of kindness. The least kind action is taller than the hugest wrong. The weakest kindness can lift a heavy weight. Kindness reaches far and wide and travels swiftly. What a beautiful entanglement of charity we get ourselves into by doing kind things! What possesses us that we do not do them oftener?

Kind actions go upon unselfish motives. They are constantly occupied when there is no hope of repayment and of a favor in return. ["The true measure of a man is how he treats someone who can do nothing for him."]

Some Rules For Kindness

It may not be out of place to lay down a few plain rules for the doing of kind actions. I have said that the majority of them require no effort; but when they are done with effort, it is unkind not to keep the effort out of view. We should never repeat to others our kind actions.

We should never dwell upon kind actions in our minds. [Wasn't that wonderful of me to do that?] ...When we are tempted to be complacent about them, let us think about the sanctity of God [and all that we have already received from all quarters] and be ashamed. Let us dwell on his attribute of magnificence and be especially devout to it. We shall thus keep ourselves within the limits of our own littleness, and even feel comfortable in them.

Be A Good Receiver

[Many people are wonderfully giving of themselves, but refuse the kindness of others. I once stopped at a convenience store. As I got out of the car, I saw a young guy holding the door for me. I called out thanks and waved him on. When I got back in the car, I was reminded that this thoughtful young man was trying to do something nice for me and that I got in the way of a kindness. Don't let pride, independence or stubbornness get in the way of the kindnesses of others. Let go. Kindnesses should be encouraged and maximized, not obstructed. Be a good receiver, as well as a generous giver.]

Lead By Example

[Set an example for your children and others to emulate. Sometimes it can be awkward to take the lead, particularly if you might be likely to face criticism for it, but when others see that your kindness comes from the heart and that the effort is effective, they may be encouraged to follow your example. As musician Charlie Parker said encouragingly: "Don't be afraid. Just play the music." When you think of something kind to do, just do it. Don't worry about criticism. You can weather it. It's also a good rule to follow for maximizing your own talents. Naturally, be considerate of the advice of others, some of which might be wise, that can help to more appropriately guide your actions.

We can set an example, even at the end. Keeping that focus can guide us in life. In my mother's final illness, she shared a room with a young mother whom I later learned had valued the time she spent with her and found her advice helpful and comforting. We can help someone, even at the

Kindness [1892] Frederick W. Faber

end from a hospital bed, not only by our words, but also by our example, and even by the way we die.

Early in the morning hours of December 12, 1988, when my mother was close to death, the nurses considerately thought it might be upsetting for her roommate and asked if she wanted to be moved to another room. She said that she wanted to stay and be with my mother. Such a selfless kindness and thoughtful repayment for the counsel my mother had offered her. Kindnesses can be extended and repaid in ways, and at times, we could never envision.

The death of loved ones is always difficult. I remember thinking when my parents and some of my friends died what a void they left. It's a worthwhile goal to try to take up the slack in some way for a good life transformed, through increased efforts of our own.]

Kind Suffering

Kind suffering is in fact a form of kind action, with peculiar rubrics of its own. But if all kindness needs grace, kind suffering needs it a hundredfold. Of a truth, those are rare natures which know how to suffer gracefully. There is a harmonious fusion of suffering and gentleness...What is more beautiful than consideration for others when we ourselves are unhappy?

What can be more unkind than to communicate our low spirits to others? To go about the world like demons, poisoning the fountains of joy. Have I more light because I have managed to involve those I love in the same gloom as myself? Is it pleasant not to see the sun shining on the mountain [and to see the happiness of others], even though we have none of it down in our valley? Oh the littleness and the meanness of that sickly appetite for sympathy which will not let us keep our tiny liliputian sorrows to ourselves!

[Look to the light and to the good you see, even if it's not your turn right now. In the meantime, keep your eye out for somebody to help. It will be a blessing to them, put your own problems into perspective and make you feel better. Service is the ultimate balm for our own wounds.] So let us hide our pains and sorrows. But while we hide them, let them be spurs within us to urge us on to all manner of overflowing kindness and sunny humor to those around us.

We must do all this unobtrusively, so as not to let others see that it is done on purpose. Hence it is that the saints keep silence in suffering. [That's why they're saints!] Suffer in silence, so as not to disquiet others. For the mere knowledge of what one suffers, is itself a suffering to those who love them.

Kindness Is Good Manners

Kindness is a very little virtue, very much a matter of natural temperament, and an affair of good manners, rather than of holy living.

The grass of the fields is better than the cedars of Lebanon. It feeds more, and it rests the eye better – that thymy, daisy eyed carpet, making earth sweet and fair and homelike. Kindness is the turf of the spiritual world...

Kindness [1892] Frederick W. Faber

"Man becomes great exactly in the degree
to which he works for the welfare of his fellow man."
– Gandhi

"This is the true joy in life, the being used for a
purpose recognized by yourself to be a mighty one."
- George Bernard Shaw
[Quoted from *Happiness* - Tal Ben-Shahar]

Chapter 4

Finding Yourself Through Others

Looking At The Big Picture

Jean Guibert and Frederick Faber provide timeless principles of kindness. Mother Teresa punctuates them in a modern context. It is easy to think that it's the function of the public sector to help the less fortunate. Mother Teresa noted however, that help from the public sector isn't as much as it should be. When speaking of bureaucracy she said: "So many signatures for such a small heart." And even when a great deal of help is given, government can't do it all. There are also always many needs that fall beyond the responsibility or ability of government, which are often better and more efficiently served by private organizations and individuals.

Mother Teresa spoke not only of physical suffering which is the first thing we think of when thinking of the less fortunate, but also of mental suffering. She said: "The biggest disease today is not leprosy or tuberculosis, but feeling unwanted…There is a terrible hunger for love. We can all experience that in our lives — the pain, the loneliness [regardless of our economic circumstances]. We must have the courage to recognize it …One of the greatest diseases is to be nobody to anybody…The most terrible poverty is loneliness and the feeling of being unloved…The hunger for love is much more difficult to remove than the hunger for bread."

Imagining Ourselves: All Alone

A *New York Times* feature article "For Lunch, a Party of One" by N.R. Kleinfield, accompanied by a poignant photo by James Estrin, showed a seventy-six year woman sitting at her kitchen table in a darkened room, with her meal in front of her with the television sitting on the table as her only company. She was sitting with her head bowed against her interwoven fingers as she said grace alone. "She qualified for the city's *Meals on Wheels* that brings a hot meal to her door five afternoons a week. The deliverer was a welcome dose of socialization to spice up her solitary existence. 'I don't have anybody visit me,' she said. 'No one comes knocking at my door, even if it's only a few minutes. You don't think you're living a hermit's life. You don't like to feel like you were running a race and you suddenly stopped. After all, do you want to talk to yourself day after day?' "

An eighty-five year old woman receiving meals, who was reported as moving about her apartment gingerly, with a four-wheeled walker and a seat said: "I look forward to getting my meal delivered. At least I get to see a live person who talks to me. What if I fall and nobody knows? I live alone and I refuse to leave."

A caring woman, who has been driving a meals delivery van for thirteen years, augmented her role by getting copies of the daily newspaper for three residents, picking up some grocery items for those who needed them and speaking to the phone company about a senior who had her phone service disconnected. She said: "These people need somebody… and someday I'll be in their shoes, so I hope there will be somebody like me there for me." As unlikely as we might think it to be, many of us could be in the same situation someday, ten, twenty or thirty years from now. Help and caring concern can help drive the wolf away from the door: "Fear knocked at the door. Love answered and no one was there."- [*10 Secrets For Success and Inner Peace* - Wayne Dyer]

Listening To Mother Teresa

"The poor you may have right in your own family. Find them. Love them…Speak tenderly to them…. It is easy to love people far away. It is not always easy to love those close to us. It is easier to give a cup of rice to relieve hunger, than it is to relieve the loneliness and pain of someone unloved in our own home. Bring love into your home, for this is where our love for each other must start….Never worry about numbers. Help one person at a time, and always start with the person nearest you."

"Let there always be kindness on your face, in your eyes, in your smile, in the warmth of your greeting. Always have a cheerful smile. Don't only give your care, but give your heart as well…Every time you smile at someone, it is an action of love, a gift to that person…I want you to be concerned about your next door neighbor. Do you know your next door neighbor?... It is a kingly act to assist the fallen...If we have no peace, it is because we have forgotten that we belong to each other."

"The poor give us much more than we give them. They're such strong people, living day to day without food, and they never curse, never complain. We don't have to give them pity or sympathy. We have so much to learn from them."

"At the end of life we will not be judged by how many diplomas we have received, how much money we have made, how many great things we have done. We will be judged by 'I was hungry and you gave me to eat, I was naked and you clothed me. I was homeless, and you took me in.' " Hungry not only for bread, but hungry for love. Naked not only for clothing – but naked of human dignity and respect. Homeless not only for want of a home of bricks – but homeless because of rejection."

A Growing Form of Cancer in America: The Working Poor

The working poor are more invisible and more numerous than those who are obviously poor. Pulitzer Prize award winning author David Shipler sheds light on their problems in his affecting book, *The Working Poor*. Most readers of this book wouldn't fall into the category of the working poor. They fall instead, into the category of those who can help them.

No one individual can cure the massive ills that contribute to the sad circumstances of the working poor, although some with influence and leadership may be able to make inroads in their own areas. Federal, state and local government leaders can make a difference with new, innovative programs.

Foresighted and tenacious celebrities, individuals and groups can make concerted efforts to produce meaningful improvements. For the rest of us, the difference we can make is to be guides, sustainers and bridge builders, especially helping those who need help at critical times, which for the working poor is frequently.

Shipler writes about the 35 million people in America, about one in every eight, who live in poverty. "The man who washes cars does not own one. The clerk who files cancelled checks at the bank has $2.02 in her own account... An inconvenience to an affluent family – minor car trouble, a brief illness, disrupted child care – is a crisis to them, for it can threaten their ability to stay employed. They spend everything and save nothing. They are always behind on their bills. They have miniscule bank accounts or none at all...Every problem magnifies the impact of the others...Each person's life is the mixed product of bad choices and bad fortune, of roads not taken and roads cut off by accident of birth or circumstance...Their personal mistakes have larger consequences..."

The human stories created by Shipler's interviews over a period of years provide a sad, touching, and sometimes hopeful tableau of the lives of the working poor. It also shows how support from kind people can help make a difference. Calling attention to the needs of others, his book is a work of exposition, concern and kindness.

It's difficult to do something about problems we don't know much about. We may think we have some idea of what it must be like to be part of the working poor. After reading Shipler's book however, it's clear that we can't begin to imagine the interwoven web of contributory factors that lead to, and further exacerbate, their problems. This book is not only a "must read" for the concerned, but for those on the brink of making decisions that can begin the slippery slide into poverty for them. Giving it to someone who needs it would be a kindness in itself.

Shipler notes that the working poor cuts across all racial and ethnic levels. Half of all poor families are headed by single women. Many of the working poor lead jumbled lives, with no plans, no future, and no hope. Unfortunately, in these unstable and unpromising conditions, future generations of children are propagated, who are often likely face the same fate. What contributes to these problems? Shipler cites lack of health insurance, poor housing, ineffective schools, unsafe neighborhoods, drug and alcohol abuse, poor nutrition, sexual abuse as children, unwanted pregnancies, absent fathers, high cost access to money through check cashing and paycheck advance agencies, and more.

You might wonder: "Who would ever use these high cost accesses to cash when money is short in the first place?" The answer is people who are desperate, who have no checking or savings accounts and who have no place else to turn. Most of us have at least some resources, or others to turn to, and fortunately haven't been desperate enough to know.

Interconnected problems bear daily down on the working poor. The famous English rhyme seems appropriate to their situation:

> "For want of a nail the shoe was lost,
> For want of a shoe the horse was lost,
> For want of a horse the rider was lost,
> For want of the rider the battle was lost,

Finding Yourself Through Others

> For want of a battle the kingdom was lost,
> And all for the want of a nail" –
> or in the case of the working poor, several nails.
> - [*Confesio Amantis(1390)* - John Gower]

Little things can not only mean a lot, they can mean everything to those with a crying need. Everyone has problems to resolve. For the working poor it is an all too frequent occurrence, but without the resources or often the education to address them effectively. Giving someone money to make a problem go away, listening and offering helpful advice, or making a phone call as a medical, educational, or social service professional, law enforcement officer or clergyman on behalf of someone else, can provide others with insight that might allow them to help or to have improved understanding of a difficult situation.

Shipler mentions how the famous best seller by Richard Carlson wisely tells us "not to sweat the small stuff." For people in normal circumstances, it's good advice. But for the working poor what would be "small stuff" to us, can often be catastrophic for them, because seemingly small things rock their boat regularly, threaten to sink it, or keep it stuck in the doldrums of despair, often with no way to escape. One woman said: "Nobody really wants to know that sometimes $2 is a significant amount, and $25 is always tremendous."

Some might say: "Well, a lot of these people are their own worst enemies." In more than a few cases that's true. "The haves and the have nots can often be traced back to the dids and the did nots":

- the ones who got an education or training, and those who didn't
- those who started with drugs or alcohol, and those who didn't
- the ones who got pregnant, or kept getting pregnant, and those who didn't
- those who had poor spending habits, bad attitudes, criminal records, and so on.

But with help, and strong personal efforts, people with disadvantages, self-created or otherwise, still turn the tide and make it. As a famous Japanese proverb says, those who have overcome obstacles have found that the way to success is that if you "fall down seven times, get up eight."

For a variety of reasons, others with self-created problems will never make it. We don't know which ones will and which ones won't. But they all have needs, many of them critical, as do their innocent children. How can the cycle be broken if no one steps forward to help?

A former courthouse in Newark, New Jersey offers a message from Henry Wadsworth Longfellow chiseled in stone, as relevant to kindness as it is to justice: "Be merciful as well as just." It's a message we can apply to our own judgments to help guide our actions. *Rambam's Ladder* mentions the wonderful, non-judgmental encouragement of Lord Chesterton: "Do not refuse your charity, even to those who have no merit but their misery."

Problems of the poor and working poor cascade. Anything that can help stop or stave that off can be a help. Effectively providing the needed nails, before the job is lost, the car breaks down, health deteriorates, or training and college classes are abandoned can help make a real difference at the right time. Making a difference for someone not only helps them, but it feels very good too. It also contributes to our own insight, happiness and personal growth.

Helping In Special Ways

Each of us is going to run head on into situations like these. We need to think creatively about how we could help.

Time for Breakfast

It might be a mutually beneficial for employers to provide a "breakfast bar" of nutritious food for their workers. If it's available for everybody, no one is stigmatized by appearing to be needy. Better nutrition could also mean improved employee health, fewer sick days and increased worker productivity.

Adoption

Adopting children is a huge commitment, but one that can make a dramatic difference in their lives. Two couples I know are among the many who have adopted. An attorney discovered that two young girls were living under unsatisfactory conditions and asked his wife if they could adopt. She agreed. Their family increased from four to six children.

A woman who had been previously married and had two adult children of her own, married a bachelor who wanted to have children. At almost fifty, she agreed and went to Romania alone, her first trip abroad, to bring a young girl and boy to the United States. My admiration for her was off the scale. They are excellent parents and live in an attractive subdivision in a rural area with an excellent school system. A complete transformation of lives and future for these children, made possible because of selfless kindness. These aren't sacrifices that everyone can or should make, but they can make a big difference.

Foster Care

Serving as a foster parent can also help children and families temporarily, in the hope that a family situation will improve, or until an adoption can be arranged.

Providing Backup: Really Providing It

One of my cousins, and his wonderful wife, had a beautiful, lively daughter who developed Fanconi's Anemia, a rare and often fatal disease that required that they take her out of the area for life saving treatments. During the months he had to be away from his job as a police detective to be with his daughter for her treatments, his fellow officers took turns covering his shifts, so he would never miss a paycheck. He told me it was a kindness they would never forget.

His fellow officers and their wives also held benefits to raise money to assist with the financial expense which accompanied their daughter's treatment. Sadly, their beloved daughter died, several days after she had become a teenager. A thousand people, including her eighth grade classmates, attended the unforgettable funeral service presided over by a priest who is our oldest cousin, who offered a beautiful and caring homily to ease the pain felt by everyone.

The Most Beautiful Memorial We Can Give: Turning Grief Into Good

Ironically, another detective my cousin worked with, who had supported them in their time of need, later described symptoms to him that his ailing daughter had. My cousin immediately recognized them as being similar to his daughter's symptoms. He encouraged his friend to have the doctor conduct appropriate tests to verify whether it was the same disease. Up to that point, the doctors had not been able to identify her ailment. The doctor told his friend that his daughter definitely did not have Fanconi's Anemia, but her father insisted upon a test for it. Against long odds, both officers who worked together had daughters who had developed the same rare illness.

My cousin was able to help his friend in his time of need because of the sad experience he and his wife had already had. He told him he should be insistent on having his daughter tested. He was able to play an important role in encouraging him to demand the test, and to contribute toward saving her life. After having a bone marrow transplant, she was deemed to be in remission.

My cousin and his wife miss their daughter every day, as any other parents who have lost a child would. The earlier words of Father Faber surely apply here, encouraging us to "see the sun shining on the mountain, and the happiness of others, even though we have none of it down in our valley."

When I asked my cousin for permission to mention their experience, he mentioned that someone had said to him: "Aren't you angry that your daughter died and that someone else's daughter lived? He told me he said to them: "Are you kiddin' me?" He said he recognized that because of the state of medical science at the time, that his daughter wasn't able to be saved, but added that he and his wife were as happy as they could be that his friend's daughter had been spared. If he and his wife could think in a kindly and unselfish way in such a tragic circumstance, we should easily be able to look with fondness and pleasure to the good that happens to others, even if things aren't going well for us at the moment.

Unplanned Leadership

Sometimes the way we serve isn't something we select, it's something that selects us. Katie Couric suffered the loss of her husband Jay Monahan, when he was diagnosed with colon cancer at age forty-one and died soon after, leaving her with two young daughters. Her way of dealing with this tragedy was to show kindness to others by working since then to encourage people to have colonoscopies and, with the help of many others, raising millions of dollars for colon cancer research, and for the Jay Monahan Center focusing on the treatment of cancers of the colon, pancreas and esophagus. [Katie's sister died from pancreatic cancer.] Katie underwent an on the air colonoscopy on *The Today Show* to encourage others to do the same. She received a Peabody Award for her presentation. She commented that she has received many letters from people who have thanked her for encouraging them to be tested because it saved their lives, or those of a loved one.

This highly accomplished woman said the benefit her effort produced is the most important thing she will ever do in her life. In spite of its foreboding reputation, a colonoscopy is simple and painless. I've had it done several times. I encourage you and those you love to do the same. It could save your life or theirs. I don't think anyone is fond of diagnostic procedures, but they sure beat cancer - literally and figuratively.

Stories like those of my cousin and his wife, and Katie Couric, bring the words of famed French Impressionist Auguste Renoir into sharp focus. Renoir suffered painful arthritis in his hands late in life. He was only able to paint by tying brushes to his crippled hands. He continued to paint day after day. When he was asked why he would endure such hardship in order to paint he said: "The pain passes, but the beauty remains." While the types of human pain I've described will never fully go away, so it can be with any pain that leads us to performing a kind act, or any pain that has to be endured in performing one.

Keeping A Student in School

Encouraging a student to stay in college or a training program can be critical to a person's life and to their family. I tell all my college students in the initial meetings of my courses that I am about to tell them the most important thing I will say to them the whole semester: "Now that you have started college, do not leave until you have obtained a four year college degree or have obtained training in a field with demand. If you don't do either of those things, you're going to put yourself at a disadvantage for the rest of your life and will be statistically likely to earn significantly less over your lifetime than those who get their degrees or meaningful training."

Students don't realize what a potentially catastrophic

decision leaving high school, college, or a substantive training program can be. One of the major factors David Shipler identified in *The Working Poor* that leads to poverty is dropping out of high school or college. He mentioned a mother in Ohio who said her daughter was in college and decided to drop out. The daughter thought it was no big deal at the time. It was. Her leaving was the beginning of her slide into poverty.

Students sometimes leave school because they're bored or because they don't like studying. Being poor and underemployed permanently, with all the attendant problems that go with it, is a whole lot worse. Unlike schooling and training, which is temporary, poverty can evolve into a life sentence without the possibility of parole.

Put Someone To The Test

Helping to arrange a counseling appointment and interest testing for students can provide a focus to serve as a motivation to succeed. I offered my students the opportunity to have extra points added to their final course grade if they went to the test center, took a nationally recognized interest test and brought me the multi-page printout they received. Then I referred them to our counseling office so they could obtain personalized, professional advice. My job isn't just to teach students about management and business law, it's also to help them gain a focus and succeed, however they choose to define success.

Colleges and universities offer free counseling and interest testing to their students and assist them in interpreting test results which can suggest career options. Interest tests are also available on the internet. Helping students with their reading and study skills can improve academic performance too. Combine that with students who apply themselves, and who don't work too many hours or abuse alcohol - other major detriments to proper academic performance - and you have a student who is positioned to succeed, and who will most likely avoid joining the working poor.

Sticking To The Basics: Providing Food

Helping provide nutritious food to a family, particularly at the end of the month, can be a huge help to families running low, as they wait for next month's assistance or food stamps to become available.

Being Loyal, Reliable and Doing The Right Thing

Doing what should be done helps someone else and it helps us, often for far longer. In discussing how loyalty is a kindness, Piero Ferrucci mentioned in *The Power of Kindness* that there was a huge snow storm in Florence, the cold was polar and things came to a standstill. But he was scheduled to give a lecture and went on foot. It took him two hours to get there. He gave the lecture to a handful of people. "When I recall it, I am glad I did it. I know I did the right thing, and I like myself for doing it...When we are loyal and reliable, we feel a fundamental integrity that gives us a sense of well-being...Always, loyalty gives substance and strength to kindness." Bear the trouble and the inconvenience that sometimes accompanies helping someone. It will only make you feel better in the end.

Giving It Away

Wilhelm Roentgen, the German physicist who discovered

the x-ray, never patented any portion of his discovery, considering it a gift to humanity. Tim Berners-Lee did the same thing with his development of the internet.

What gifts can we give to humanity? If you offer a professional or technical service, give it away to those you can who need it. Many thoughtful and caring legal and medical practitioners already do. Others do the same in diverse fields. Mechanics and craftspeople cut some people a break on their repair bills. Others volunteer their labor or provide materials to construct or repair recreation facilities or historic sites.

Many other suggestions appear in a subsequent section of the book. The better understanding someone has of needs in the community, and of particular individuals and families, including their own, the more ways that will be envisioned to help.

> "Everything that is not given is lost."
> -Indian proverb

Chapter 5

Conflicting Thoughts On Kindness

Many occasions for kindness present themselves daily. The question is whether we are going to initiate kind acts in response to them. They can easily be ignored because of lack of time, not seeing it as our responsibility, because of selfishness or for other reasons.

But what about kind people who would think of helping, but have conflicts about whether they should or shouldn't? This is a good place not to skim. Even if the headings that follow initially hold little initial interest for you, it will be very helpful to read the content. It contains some heartwarming stories and many broader, worthwhile thoughts.

Its None of My Business

There may be a tendency to just jump in and try to offer advice, service or money, but then we might think that it's not our affair. If we decide to act, we run the risk of being turned down, or being more firmly rebuffed, but in those cases, it's probably worth taking the risk anyway. It's better to develop a thicker skin and not to take any rejections personally. Better to take a knock now and then, than to risk having someone who needs help going without it.

When there is more time for reflection, it might help to bring the matter to the attention of someone else whom you believe to be wiser or better suited to the task, providing assistance to them if necessary, or acting yourself, if it seems as if no action is going to be taken and should be.

If the opportunity seems to be left to you, why are you the one who should help? The only answer is, "because destiny put you in this place in history, in this moment in time, and the task is yours to do." - British Prime Minister Tony Blair [speaking in a different context]

"Even the smallest person can change the course of the future" [*The Lord of the Rings*.] What a powerful thought. Even if we don't have much money or much time, even if we are elderly or in ill health or dying, even if we haven't done much to help others in the past, we can make a real difference in someone else's life, and possibly in our own too, which can change their lives and disclose some essential truths about our own.

I Don't Have Time

In *A Short Course on Kindness,* Margot Silk Forrest says: "Time is one of the biggest enemies of kindness." But even a busy person has time to check behind them to see if someone's coming and to hold the door for them. Many people are so self-absorbed, and sometimes so thoughtless, forgetful or in a hurry, that they just blast through a door with no concern about who's behind them. How much extra time does it take? Three seconds? It's difficult to conceive that would materially throw someone off schedule. Just a simple act like this is something people appreciate - that someone took the time to do something for them, to show them a sign of respect, particularly if they're already loaded down with books, packages or have children in hand. When I was in France, coming into a department store, a woman held the door for me, a custom I didn't find common there. I said, "Merci." She simply replied, "Rien." - the equivalent of "It's nothing." That's how much trouble it is.

Once we see the good we're doing, we'll see more opportunities and realize many of them hardly impinge on our time at all. The gain in the good feeling it creates will more than compensate for the few moments someone might "lose" by the end of the day.

I'm Too Busy

There probably aren't too many people who would use these exact words, but some people's self-absorbed behavior can reflect it.

Former heavyweight champion George Foreman was admittedly an unpleasant and self-centered man in his earlier years. Its hard to imagine that he's the same smiling face we've seen on television many times, a man who left boxing to begin a ministry and who started programs to benefit young people.

In his book, *George Foreman's Guide to Life,* Foreman says: "You shouldn't be afraid to change; instead, be afraid to stay where you are in life... People seem to forget completely that you bring nothing into this world and you won't take anything out either – nothing, that is, but the love and respect you've earned throughout your life and the memories of what you've done for others."

"Not in his goals, but in his transitions is a man great...A noble man compares and estimates himself by an idea higher than himself; and a mean[average] man, by one lower than himself. The one produces aspiration; the other ambition, which is the way a vulgar man aspires...And you will find rest from vain fancies, and will give relief to yourself, if you do every act of your life as if it is your last... Let men see, let men know, a real man, who lives as he was meant to live... It is not death a man should fear, but he should fear never beginning to live." [*Meditations*, Marcus Aurelius]

Marcus Aurelius also noted that his secretary, Alexander the Platonist, advised him against frequently using the words "I am too busy" in speech or correspondence, except in cases of real necessity; saying no one ought to regularly shirk the obligations due to society on the excuse of urgent affairs.

Too much business, not enough concern? Marcus Aurelius' *Meditations* suggests what our focus should be: "Let [reason] play the part of the slave no more, twitching puppet like at every pull of self-interest...Guard also against another kind of error: the folly of those who weary their days in much business, but lack any aim on which their whole effort, nay their whole thought is focused...Man has but one life; already yours is nearing its close, yet still has no eye to your own honor." [It's sobering to remember that not only are terminal patients dying. We all are. I've seen many occasions when those who were ill or aged themselves attended funerals for those far younger or those not expected to die. We should allocate our time accordingly.]

Joel Osteen in *Your Best Life Now* says: "If you want to live your best life now, you must develop a lifestyle of "living to give, instead of living to get…To catch monkeys years ago, hunters would take a large barrel and fill it with bananas… Then they'd cut a hole in the side, just large enough that the monkey could barely get his arm through it. The monkey would reach in the barrel and grab one of those treats. But when he clenched his fist, it would be too large to back out of the hole. The monkey would be so stubborn and so intent on holding on to what he had in his hand, even when his captors converged on him, he wouldn't turn it loose. He was easy prey for the men with the nets. Sadly, monkeys are not alone when it comes to selfishness. Many people… live with their hands clenched. They are focused on holding on to what they have [or on getting more]…They are selfish with their money, with their resources and with their time. Those who live life in this way abandon the many silent thrills and blessings they could enjoy, and the improved self-esteem and happiness they could find, if they stepped into the breach to help others."

The Dhammapada, a compendium of the major themes of Buddhist thought similarly says: "Ambition and acquisition are inferior routes to happiness…He can live in joy, when master of himself, by the edge of the forest of desires."

The Dalai Lama points out further that: "Ruthless people can never relax. The compassionate have freedom of mind and peace…when a man forgets to cultivate his inner life, he turns himself into a machine and becomes a slave to material things. Then he is a human being in name only…

and those who are brought up in such an atmosphere will find themselves lacking all their lives: they will not know that wonderful quality of depth and intimacy that is the richness of life. They will stay on the surface of the troubled sea, without ever knowing the calm that lies beneath."

As things stand now, can you honor your life? "If you have not felt the joy of doing a kind act, you have neglected much, most of all yourself. It is possible to give away and become richer! It is also possible to hold on too tightly and lose everything."

"Happiness is not attained through self-gratification, but through fidelity to a worthy purpose." - Helen Keller. The more you grasp, the less you have - and the less you are. What worthy difference can you make?

If I Give Money To A Street Person, How Do I Know He Isn't Going To Buy Alcohol Or Drugs Or That He's Not Trying to Scam Me?

Well you don't. Certainly you don't want to feel like part of supporting an alcohol or drug habit, or just plain laziness. When I was younger, I asked my father about it and he told me that it was his job to give. What people did with the money afterward was up to them. I guess I've followed that line of thinking ever since.

Whether someone is a scammer is a matter of judgment. Sometimes it's a "no brainer." I was in New York City near 60th and Amsterdam. On a stone cold day, not too far from Lincoln Center, I saw a poorly dressed man laying down in the afternoon on the sidewalk for some sleep on a piece of cardboard, pulling a ragged piece of filthy cloth over himself. He did it as naturally as we would lie down on a sofa and pull a quilt up over us. It was patently obvious that he had a need.

A few days after I saw the man in New York, I was walking in Philadelphia and a guy about thirty-five was lazily leaning against a building holding a plastic bag and an umbrella that seemed to be in pretty good shape. He said: "Can you spare some change for a cup of coffee?" It's not uncommon to come across such situations without warning and to have to make a decision almost instantly. I didn't give him anything. He may have had some need, but he looked a little too good, clearly capable of doing more to help himself.

Another day a man came up to me in Philadelphia and said: "Mister, I'm really hungry. I haven't had anything to eat all day." I had some doubts about the depth of his need, but he used words I couldn't ignore. Give to those who you feel have a need. Some selectivity is needed. We can't give to everyone. And we don't want to give to those who clearly don't need it. You'll make some mistakes in judgment as I have, but don't let it deter you from giving. The overall impact of your giving will be beneficial.

Why Should I Give Anything To These People? Why Don't They Just Go Out And Get A Job?

Most of us have a reasonable degree of education, skills and stability in our lives and are not plagued by the health problems, mental illness, sexual abuse, development of bad habits, the traumatic stress of veterans, the distractions to clear thinking caused by excessive drug or alcohol abuse, or a myriad of other circumstances which led someone to find themselves on the street, or otherwise disadvantaged. Most of us are also fortunate enough to have a job.

When I was about ten, my parents, my sister and I were riding over to Philadelphia to visit my grandfather. As soon as we crossed the bridge from New Jersey, I saw some shabbily dressed men just sitting around in the park and said: "Look at those bums." My father just said quietly: "There go I, but for the grace of God." Over fifty years later, I remember that comment as if it were yesterday. It wasn't my place to judge, then or now.

Recently, I read that a wise woman went one better and commented that the proper frame of mind shouldn't be: "There go I, but for the grace of God", but simply: "There go I", a human being just like me with feelings and needs - needs we might be able to address.

Julie Salamon, author of *Rambam's Ladder* offers a memorable example of this. She said she had a cartoon from *The New Yorker* on her wall in which "a prosperous man with a briefcase, mouth set grimly, is ignoring a stubble-faced fellow holding out his hat. The man asking for the handout looks annoyed and says: 'It's not as if I'm asking you to acknowledge our common humanity.' " No he wasn't, but it's something we can acknowledge with everyone we meet, regardless of their station in life.

Rather than judging, and being so sure of the certainty of our analysis, it might be better to just cut the potential recipient some slack, and do what we can to help and leave the rest up to them. It's not an easy journey. It's a long road and a slippery slope. A few lifts along the way might be helpful.

Conflicting Thoughts On Kindness

I Fought My Way Up. Let People Take Care of Their Own Problems Like I Did.

Anyone who has overcome adversity to get where they are is to be admired. They have succeeded when most others in similar circumstances haven't. That's what makes them noteworthy. Maybe some of those who didn't make it didn't get the money, help, advice or concern they needed at the right times. Maybe some of them had personal or addictive weaknesses that those who made it didn't have. Maybe they just developed a pattern of laziness or criminal behavior at an early age and never got rid of it. Those who have faced challenges like these on the road to success have an understanding of these things that most of us never will. Such insights are better utilized by making a difference, not by judging.

Sometimes this can happen in unexpected ways. And sometimes it is the young that lead us. *More Random Acts of Kindness* contains many stories about how acts of kindness affected the lives of others. A man said he managed to screw up his life so badly that he found himself homeless. He said he was so absorbed in self-pity that all he could think of was begging, so he could buy his next drink: "One day I was panhandling when a woman walked by with a small boy in tow. She ignored my pitch and hurried away. As I watched them go down the sidewalk, the small boy broke free and came running back. He stood in front of me, fumbling in his coat pocket. He pulled out a five-dollar bill that was certainly more money than he had ever had before, and handed it to me. I was completely dumbstruck and just sat there staring at him with the money in my hand. By then his mother had returned and, with tears in her eyes, gently led the boy away. He turned back once to wave and they were gone. I don't know how long I sat there, but I have not had another drink since then." We never know the power of influence we can have or why things happen as they do. Sometimes, it's not for us to know.

You never know which one of your kindnesses will make a substantive difference. Just keep throwing them up against the wall. Some of them will stick for a long time and make a real difference. As in teaching, sometimes you never get to know what kind of an impact you may have made. The motivation has to be to just do the right thing and trust that it will help.

I Need To Get Help, Not Give It.

The Talmud reminds us: "Even a poor man, a recipient of charity, should give charity." By giving, whether it's money or of ourselves, we add to our self-worth when we see we can help someone else, no matter how little we have ourselves. Our insights into the kind of poverty we face, be it financial or emotional, can also help us better understand what someone in a similar situation might be going through and need just then. A rising tide raises all ships - theirs and yours.

There could hardly be a better example of giving by the poor than the stories told about the victims of the great tsunami in the Indonesia/Thailand region. An experienced and respected British reporter for one of the major news networks said he was truly touched when he saw people who had lost everything, including their spouses and children, sharing their meager food rations with foreigners and tourists. If they could do that in the horrific situations they faced, we can share in any comparatively minimal sad states that we might find ourselves.

When we're feeling impotent, nothing can help repair a self image better, than to know that we still have power - the power to help make things better for someone else, even if we can't seem to get it done for ourselves just then. I call it "The Moses Effect." Moses led others to The Promised Land, but he couldn't enter himself. Sometimes we can help others out of the wilderness, even if it's not our time yet. There is a healing in helping. If things get bad for you, find someone to help. You'll not only help them, but will be taking a positive step on the road to getting yourself out of your own dilemma and moving toward becoming whole again.

People Often Don't Appreciate What's Done For Them, So Why Should I Bother Helping Them?

A true gift is given without any expectation of something in return. It's nice when appreciation is shown, but the mental state of the receiver might be such that they're not thinking clearly in the normal way that most of us do - or at least think we do! The good comes from the doing. We can only control what we do, not the reaction we get. We just have to have enough conviction and confidence in ourselves to know we've done the right thing and take any feedback we get to help us improve our approach.

"Life means being happy and making others happy.
The first gift is a smile and listening."
-Soeur Emanuelle
[A French nun renowned for her kindness]

Your Unfinished Life

> "What have I learned
> Where 'er I've been,
> From all I've heard
> From all I've seen?
> What know I more worth knowing?
> What have I done that's worth the doing?
> What have I sought that I should shun?
> What duties have I left undone?"
> - Pythagoras

> "When your cup is full, stop pouring."
> - Lao Tsu

Chapter 6

You Can Make A Difference

French Renaissance philosopher Michel de Montaigne noted: "The great and glorious masterpiece of man is to live with purpose." "Without a high purpose, a calling [where the work is an end in itself], or an ideal, we cannot attain our full potential for happiness." [*Happiness* -Tal Ben Shahar] It's up to us to discover what works for us. Shahar's book, and others mentioned in the resources section at the end of this book, can help you identify your own high purposes that can lead you to happiness.

"Difficulties Are Things That Show What Men Are" - Epictecus

I saw a man sitting on the sidewalk outside a Burger King in Center City Philadelphia late in the afternoon on Christmas Eve day. I asked him if he wanted some clothes I had been keeping in the car for someone who might have been able to use them. He accepted them willingly. I also gave him an amount of money I had never given before, one I don't think he saw too often. If perhaps you're thinking: "Wasn't that nice?", I want to assure you that I was the one who came out way ahead in the encounter that day.

When I gave this gentleman the folded up money as I shook his hand, he opened it up, looked at it, then he looked at me and said: "Do you know how much you gave me?" I said that I did. He thanked me, we had a brief conversation, then I left. I thought to myself afterward, here's a man sitting on a sidewalk, on a cold December day, with next to nothing, and when someone gives him something he clearly needed, he had the character to ask if I had given him what I intended. He may have been down on his luck, but he was right there with his principles. What explains how a man who has virtually nothing, shows character to emulate, and how others who have so much already will go to any length to get more, even when it's to the detriment of others?

Be An Honorable Recipient

Some might wonder what this man did with the money. Of course, I'll never know. But it was given with the belief that it would be used for something he thought was beneficial. All of us receive from others in one way or another. Are we good stewards of the gifts we receive? We can make a difference not only by what we give, but also by the level of responsibility we take for what we've received.

Students who are having their tuition paid, in whole or part, owe their best efforts to dignify the assistance that's been given. Those who are given or loaned money to help them, should use the money for expected purposes. Likewise, we should use the talents we've been given, in repayment for the fact that we're fortunate enough to have them.

Kindnesses should also be repaid to the giver, if that was the understanding. A woman I know and her late husband encouraged a young man who had dropped out of a fine college to complete his education after returning back East. They lent him a substantial sum of money so he could. A number of years later when they asked him to repay the money because they needed it to help educate one of their own children, he refused to repay them anything, saying that one of his parents had helped the husband in the past and that their making him the loan was repayment of that. Not only a breach of faith, but a double fault.

My father tutored many men and women to help them pass their state mortuary licensing examinations. He also helped some of them obtain loans to finance the start of their businesses. Several of them told me how grateful they were because they felt they would never have become funeral directors without his help. If I had ever gone to any of these people asking for something "because of what my Dad did for you", my father would not only have been disgraced by my actions, he would rightly have thought a whole lot less of me as a human being for misappropriating his good name. Unless it was agreed to in advance, we shouldn't expect recompense for our own kindnesses, and certainly never for those of others.

Safety First

For your own security, never allow a stranger who needs help for any reason to follow you to your home or car, to get into your car, or allow them entrance to your home. You might think, "Who would ever do something like that?" Just ask the police.

If you give any money on the street, have it readily available for the purpose in a pocket, rather than having to open a wallet or purse, which could lead to an assault or theft. It's never good judgment to be flashing money around at any time, or to risk your own personal security or those who are with you. It is also important to be as discreet as possible to preserve the dignity of the recipient. But always safety first. If it's not safe, don't help. You'll have other opportunities.

Be All You Can Be

The US Army used this theme to great effect in its advertising, recognizing that it's an innate desire many people have. Famed social scientist Abraham Maslow said we are motivated by a hierarchy or ranked ordering of needs, the highest of which is self-actualization or self-realization, working toward becoming our idealized self – "What a man can be, he must be."

Your past doesn't have to be your present and your future. There is always time to be the person you were destined to be. The actor Robert Forster, a comeback actor who received an Academy Award nomination credited it with re-starting his long acting career. He remarked appropriately at the time: "You can still win it in the late innings."

And so it is with all of us. Nido Qubein and *Reader's Digest* reported the following anecdote by George Bernard Shaw: "Mr. Shaw was asked by a reporter, ' If you could live your life over and be anybody you've known, or be any person from history, who would it be? ' Shaw replied: ' I would choose to be the man George Bernard Shaw could have been, but never was.' "Because we all have unique gifts, no one else can be exactly the same type of good and caring person you can be. As Emerson said: "Insist on yourself. Never imitate."

"Of all the words of tongue or pen, the saddest are these, it might have been." Who could you have been? You still can be. "Find the place of peace and joy. Don't live the horror of the half filled life." -Wayne Dyer

Do you want to go ahead, not knowing who you truly are and what you might have become? Was there ever a grieving parent who has lost a child, or a couple that never had one, that didn't wonder what their child's life would have been like? You are the prospective parent of your own fulfilled self. Don't wonder what might have been. Visualize your best life. Then live it. As Robert Schuller says: "The me that you see is the me you will be."

We can all look back over our lives and recall truly exciting moments that gave us satisfaction. It is as if we've found our place and now know how we can leave our mark. Herman Melville talks about this kind of discovery when he says: "It is not down on any map, true places never are." It is the things we find we have a passion for. "A bird does not sing because it has an answer. It sings because it has a song." - Maya Angelou.

Some of us find our place at an early age. For others, it takes longer. My father was a man of many expressions and had a good memory for poetry. One of the poems he mentioned to me many times is appropriate to the journey of finding ourselves. It ended by saying that eventually we "stumbleth at last to our suitable place." That place includes

how we learned to be kind, to serve and to discover our true selves. "The only ones among you who will really be happy are those who have sought and found how to serve."
- Albert Schweitzer

We can not only make a difference when we're here, but even after we go ahead through the legacy we leave. A legacy of kindness is the golden thread by which kind words and actions from previous generations have set an example for us, and how our kindnesses will be part of a legacy that can influence those who follow.

John van Hengel left just such a legacy. *The New York Times* in reporting his death: "John van Hengel, 83, Dies; Set Up First Food Bank in U.S." identified him also as the person who established "Second Harvest", a national organization to spread the food banking concept. From a modest beginning, that organization distributed nearly two billion pounds of food to more than 50,000 local charitable agencies in the previous year.

It all started when he spoke with a woman who had ten children, and a husband on death row, who said she fed her family by salvaging usable food from refuse bins behind a local grocery store. This caused him to ask the manager if he could take such food and dented cans to help the less fortunate. That manager and others agreed. He later helped spread the concept of food banking to Canada, Europe and Africa. As reporter Douglas Martin noted in his story: "A man searching for purpose had found one." And what a legacy he left.

A simple man with modest means made a huge difference. What is your purpose? How can we use our powers of observation and our talents to do what is beneficial in similar or smaller spheres?

> "You don't get to choose how you're going to die.
> Or when. You can only decide how
> you're going to live. Now."
> - Joan Baez
> [Quoted from *A Short Course on Kindness*]

Chapter 7

40 Ways To Be Kind

James Hollis in *Finding Meaning in the Second Half of Life*, commenting on Carl Jung, says: "It is far easier to walk in shoes too small for us than to step into the largeness that the soul expects and demands. Much unhappiness is caused by the refusal to step out of our own littleness."

The number of ways to step forward is infinite. In her research, Sonja Lyubomirsky determined that when finding meaning from a higher purpose, "different methods are a better fit for different people." ["The Way To Happiness" by Dianne Hales, *Reader's Digest*]

There are many suggestions below. All of them won't be you. Choose some that are or develop your own that are suited to your unique talents and personality.

There are helpful thoughts in each section that follows. Even if the headline doesn't seem to apply to you, it's best to read all of this, as tempted as you may be to skim.

You can't go wrong with anything good you do in

moderation. Just align it with whatever signature strengths and inner purposes you have in your life and let your actions express that. As Eckhart Tolle says in *The New Earth:* "See yourself inspiring countless people with your work and enriching their lives."

Don't be concerned about equaling or surpassing anyone in particular, only meeting your own high expectations of yourself. "We often enhance our happiness to the greatest extent when we pursue activities that provide us with meaning and pleasure *and* that help others." [*Happiness* - Tal Ben Shahar]

Lyubomirsky in *The How of Happiness* reveals that a person's level of happiness is primarily determined by three factors:

- a genetically determined set point for happiness that accounts for about 50% of our happiness
- happiness relevant circumstantial factors such as marriage, money, level of education and the like, which accounts for only about 10% of happiness
- happiness relevant activities and practices which account for about 40% of happiness

We can't change our genes, and the circumstantial factors don't have much overall influence on happiness levels. What we can influence though is what we spend our time doing, so we should choose wisely. Most people fall far short of their potential for happiness because they misuse precious time.

Try to simplify your life as much as possible, by eliminating unnecessary activities and properly prioritizing those that remain. Delegate to others whenever you can. This not only frees up time, but it also clears your head to make room for higher order thoughts and goals.

A cluttered mind is an inefficient mind. You will think more clearly and will be better able to focus on what's truly important when you reduce the number of competing thoughts and concerns. It's analogous to picking up extraneous things from the floor before you start vacuuming. While having a variety of activities can be desirable, it's better to focus your energy on one thing at a time as much as possible. It has been shown to be a more effective way of operating, despite the braggadocio about how good some people say they are at multi-tasking.

1. Kindness Made Simple

In *Living Faith*, Jimmy Carter relates the charge of Reverend Eloy Cruz: "You have only two loves in your life - for God and for the person in front of you." [If you don't believe in God, then just take care of the person in front of you.] "Within my own talent and realm of possibilities, what can I find to do that would be good and lovely?" – Mother Teresa

Deepak Chopra in *The Seven Laws of Spiritual Success* simplifies kindness: "Give wherever you go to whomever you see... Ask how you can help, not what's in it for me."

My parents lie buried next to each other. Their grave markers lie flat on the ground, my father's on the left and my mother's on the right. My sister suggested that my father's marker say: "This is the day the Lord has made...", the balance of which is the implied "let us rejoice and be glad", one of my father's favorite quotations. In honor of all the charitable work my mother did, my late and gifted brother-in-law suggested that her marker use an expression of Mother Teresa's: "Do something beautiful for God." One day when I was standing there looking down, it struck me all of a sudden that reading their markers straight across, it read: "This Is The Day the Lord Has Made...Do Something Beautiful For God." Challenged, even from the grave. My sister and me - and maybe you too.

If you like dreams, you'll like this. Ironically my sister, a kind and caring hospital chaplain in Michigan, said that she had a dream in which my father said to "Appreciate every day" and my mother said, "Do it now." I guess their epitaphs were well chosen.

2. Be There For Someone Who Is Sick or Grieving

It's nice to know you're thought of when you're sick. Inquire whether someone would welcome a hospital or home visit. It's also important not to stay too long, unless you're invited to stay longer. Anyone recovering needs rest. That's hard to come by if there are too many visitors.

Make a call, send a card, or send some flowers. See if there is anything practical you can do, such as bringing a meal to those still at home or cleaning the house.

It's also very important to maintain contact with people who mean something to you, even if you only ask others about them. Someone whose welfare I cared about died after an extended illness. I had not even known she was sick. Sometimes we just lose contact or get involved in our own lives. Sometimes we may just keep to ourselves too much. Learning about a death and going to a funeral is far from an acceptable substitute to extending a kindness when the person is still living. Think about those who mean something to you who you don't see often and contact them, or at least find out how they're doing.

When there has been a death, attend the viewing to offer condolences to the family. It means a lot, even if you haven't seen the family members, or the deceased, for a long time. Sometimes the longer the time has been, and the greater the distance traveled, the greater the impact. Family and close friends are expected to come to funerals. They offer wonderful support at a time when it's needed. When someone comes who wasn't expected though, it can give loved ones an extra boost.

Don't worry about "not knowing what to say." They know why you're there and they know you're sorry. Just give them a warm handshake or a hug and tell them something nice about their loved one. Or tell them that you'll pray for them and their family, if that's a comment appropriate for them and for you.

Write a personal note to a deceased's spouse, partner, parents or children. People can feel awfully lonely in the times after funeral services, when others have gone back to their normal routines. Just write from the heart. Keep it positive and uplifting.

Don't say at a viewing, or write: "He/she's better off" or "It was God's will" unless you are absolutely certain such a sentiment will have a comforting impact. Those who grieve may come to that kind of thinking later, but most people don't want to hear it when they've just suffered a loss, particularly if the death was sudden or involved the loss of a child. Be more concerned about being kind, than philosophizing about what you think is "right."

People are sometimes reluctant to call or visit a relative

or good friend who has just suffered the loss of a loved one: "I don't want to bother her now" or "He won't want company." Let that up to them. Take the risk. They may be lonely and buried in sad thoughts. That feeling can be compounded when people stop calling because they're afraid to. It isn't uncommon for people who have lost loved ones to be effectively treated like lepers for a while. It is far from helpful to them. Wait a few weeks, then call and ask if they'd like to talk, like a visit, or would like to go out to lunch, then follow their lead. Getting someone in this situation out of the house can also be very helpful by assisting them in changing perspective.

If you are the one who is grieving, don't wait for others to call you. Call friends and ask them to come over and see you, to meet in the park to go for a walk or to meet for lunch or dinner. They'll come. Your calling will overcome any reluctance they may have had to call you. It will also help re-establish normal relations again and will help give you some of the support you need.

3. Provide Love and Support for the Dying

Trying to provide support to someone who is dying is a delicate undertaking and not one suited to everyone. Certainly anyone can, at the least, send a thoughtful card to share positive and personal thoughts with someone who is terminally ill.

Under these circumstances, if someone feels he/she would like to visit, they should call first to ask the person, or their family, if it's all right to come. Any visit should be kept fairly short and geared to the needs of the person who is ill. Ask the caregiver if there is anything you can do to help them. They need help and support too. Big time.

A few special people can provide love and support right until the end. For the person who is sick, this time has to have some apprehension at the least. If yours is a presence that's desired, it can make a positive contribution to peacefulness. It's a unique opportunity to be there at a time when you're really needed. Just being there to listen can be comforting.

I know of several circumstances where the person providing support instinctively knew the time to act near the end, or was asked to act, and got into bed next to the person nearing transition and just held them and talked to them lovingly and supportively until they passed. It is hard to envision a more affecting situation, or one when someone would need to palpably feel the love and support of another human being more.

It is also a special gift to others to provide support to the dying through hospice care. If one feels called to this, and if hospice administrators feel someone can offer support in an acceptable way, it is an act of kindness that is as special as one can get. Even if one is not called to such service, hospice programs always need and appreciate financial and other support.

4. Help Those In Sudden Need

If you see someone on the evening news, or in the newspaper, who has faced a tragedy and needs money or other help, call the station or the newspaper to find out how you can send something to them. Write a letter of support to accompany your gift. It can be particularly meaningful if you have already undergone the same difficulty they are now facing whether it's a sudden death in the family, a fire or some other tragedy. If you have, be sure to mention it. A message from someone who's "been there" creates a special kinship. Tell them to call or e-mail you if they'd like to talk, if that's something you'd feel comfortable doing. If you've been there yourself, you'll know even better what to say and how to say it.

More Random Acts of Kindness shows how powerful the communication of a pressing need can be: "I drive a taxicab in San Diego and have seen thousands of acts of kindness. One of the most wonderful came when the stepfather of our dispatcher died, and the dispatcher could not afford the airfare to fly back to New Jersey for the funeral. All day long, the pledges of money kept coming in over the radio. It was just like a private telethon. Cab drivers and even passengers who heard what was happening over the radio started emptying their pockets. We raised the plane fare in no time." All it takes is a prime mover to get the ball rolling.

5. Broadcast Highly Defined Needs/DonorsChoose.org

When you know there's a real need, try to "broadcast" it in some way by contacting television, radio stations, "action lines" or websites. The media is a powerful source to communicate pressing needs to others. The problem is rarely with the size of people's hearts. More often it's with their not being aware of the need. That's where you can come in. Never presume someone else will do it. Diffused responsibility often becomes no responsibility.

Not long before a Christmas past, *The Courier-Post* newspaper in Southern New Jersey ran three articles, the last one entitled "Destitute Family Stays Together." The family of ten, a mother and father in their early thirties, and eight children between the ages of one and thirteen had fallen through the cracks of the welfare system and were facing the placement of the children in foster care because their subsidized time in a two room motel unit, and money, was running out. The husband was on disability. His wife had a job near minimum wage. Ultimately, through the efforts of their church, the county's transitional services and largely through the efforts of the newspaper and the three reporters who worked on the story, the family was able to get help at the eleventh hour. The day after the first story ran, the newspaper reported that the family had received over fifty e-mails offering housing, money, clothing and other help.

In a similar, but less urgent vein, there are probably few examples of how to connect needs with those who want to do something positive, than the website *www.DonorsChoose.org* : "Every teacher a grant-writer. Every citizen a philanthropist."

This site, started by Charles Best, a New York City schoolteacher, allows teachers from around the country to write proposals for what they need to help their public school students. Mr. Best, in an interview with Ann Curry on *The Today Show* called it "the charity of the future", an approach that should be imitated by other organizations. Donors respond much better to specific, clearly identified needs that touch and motivate them, than they do to broad appeals.

The site itself is one you would find interesting to visit. It is elegantly simple. A teacher writes a description of what is needed to assist students. Potential donors simply click on the donor button and a list of projects appears, categorized by area of interest: arts, athletics, sciences, etc., then a donor can fund all or a portion of the identified need. A bar chart shows what percentage of money has been raised to date to meet the goal.

The key to this approach, for any charity or cause that needs to be served, is to be as specific as possible about what is desired and to list the needs one by one in a categorical fashion.

How could you take and adapt this idea to help your high school, church, community, job bank, or whatever else you can think of, to meet pressing needs? The internet is one of the most powerful tools on earth. It has unlimited potential for doing good and extending kindness.

Mr. Best was motivated to begin his site when he discovered that basic tools needed to teach students were lacking due to budgetary and other problems. The funding needed was often modest. One teacher simply needed pencils for students. A donor saw the request on *DonorsChoose.org* and supplied the requisite sixty dollars to buy them. Educational class trips, book purchases and a twenty thousand dollar playground have also been similarly funded.

Another teacher received funding to provide a smoke detector for each student to take home, after one of their classmates died in a home fire. Wherever there's a need, there's a way. Find a need and fill it, whether you do it through *Donors Choose* or in some other way. Think inside the box, and outside of it.

6. Write A Note of Condolence To The Family of a Deceased Veteran, Police Officer or Firefighter

No matter what someone's views may be on specific wars

and military actions, people have traditionally been strong supporters of their country and military service personnel. It is a great sadness to see anyone lose his or her life tragically, particularly when they are pledged to serving all of us. Such losses are tragic at any age, but particularly at a young age, before they had much opportunity to live full lives of their own, or at an age when spouses, partners, minor children and parents are left behind. Telling the families of our military, police and firefighters how much you appreciated their loved one's service and how deeply sorry you are for the great loss they are suffering can help a little, particularly when it is coming from a total stranger.

7. Give Someone A Ride To The Store Or To The Doctor's Office

Some people can only take a bus to get somewhere. Some can't even do that because there is no public transportation near them, or because of illness or advanced age. Anyone you can take somewhere can often use some company too. Being without transportation can obviously contribute to social isolation.

8. Combat Loneliness: Visit An Elderly Neighbor

Let your friends and neighbors know about it too, so they can help out if they wish. If you are able, it's also nice to have an elderly person visit your home for lunch or tea. It provides a change of scenery for them, so they don't have to keep looking at the same four walls all day.

It would be such a helpful thing if people throughout the country would establish toll free, phone lines manned by volunteers who could just talk to seniors and the homebound who are lonely. It could also be a source of referring needs to other individuals and agencies who could assist them with problems they have, from not having enough to eat, to dealing with utility and other companies, who seniors sometimes find confusing to deal with. It would be wonderful for anyone who needed to, to just be able to pick up the phone and have a friend on the other end answer: "Hello, *We Care*, how are you today?" If you're looking for something that could make a difference for senior citizens in your community, why not give something like this a try?

9. Invite Someone Who Doesn't Have Anyone For A Meal

This is a good thing to do anytime, especially at holiday times when people are particularly lonely. No one can know how it feels to be completely alone on a holiday until they've experienced it. One woman who was alone got the idea to invite other people who were alone to come together for a holiday dinner. A creative idea that helped everyone.

My kind and thoughtful daughter Sharon worked as a home health aide for a man in his eighties. He had a daughter who had taken care of him, but she suffered a debilitating stroke, was confined to the county hospital and subsequently died. Since he had no one, we invited him for Christmas dinner. He was pleasant and appreciative. It was nice to have him. It was his last Christmas. He died two months later. Sometimes saying, "maybe next week, next month, next year, next time" isn't going to work. It might be too late by then. Do it before you count to three.

10. Lend An Empathetic Ear

We all have had times when we had to deal with the trials of life, physical, emotional or otherwise, even when some of the problems may have been caused by our own doing. Having someone being willing to listen to us at times like these, who try to put themselves in our place, can be a great help. Piero Ferrucci in *The Power of Kindness:* "Empathy is a means at our disposal for bringing relief and contentment to another person...When at last they feel that someone identifies with their experience, in that moment they are able to let go of their suffering and are healed."

My physician knows how to listen. He's a true healer of the spirit, as well as the body. On my first visit, I asked him "How long do I have?" Immediately he said: "We have as long as you need." And he meant it. Whenever I go for an appointment, it's not uncommon to wait forty-five minutes or longer. You'd think that would make someone impatient, particularly me. But I know he's spending whatever time is necessary with the patients ahead of me and, when I get to see him, he'll do the same for me. People can be true gifts to one another. He has been one to me and to many other patients. It's a long way from just being allotted an assigned block of time and being quickly moved along like a car on an assembly line.

Whether in professional practice, on your job, or on your own time, you can be the ears and the positive force that someone needs in their life, whether you're a physician, a store clerk, wait staff, nurse, attorney or bank teller. When someone is able to spend even two or three more minutes with those who need it, it can make a world of difference to them, and to those that are doing the serving too, as they discover facets of their own personalities they didn't know existed. As Stephen Covey wisely suggests in *The Seven Habits of Highly Successful People*, in managing your time, it's better to be "efficient with things and effective with people," not the other way around.

Two of my high school friends of almost fifty years, and two of my faculty colleagues, have also truly been "friends in need, friends in deed." What a blessing to know that there are people you can turn to when you need to, who care about you, no matter what problems you have, even those we may have contributed to ourselves. This type of kindness is something most of us can offer, whether it is to our family, friends or acquaintances. "A true friend is one who believes in you after he sees you at your worst."

11. Spearhead An Effort To Meet A Need

Initiate or participate in efforts to get a traffic light, crossing guard, walking or bike trails, no kill animal shelters, whatever seems important to you.

Sometimes there are larger needs, even monumental ones. It always takes someone to begin. Gutzon Borglum started carving the faces on Mt. Rushmore knowing that he wouldn't live to see the project completed. Martin Luther King said prophetically that he might not live long enough to see the dreams he described for "The Promised Land" being fulfilled. But he, along with many others in worthwhile endeavors provided the vision to change the lives of many. The road might seem long, but good gets accomplished along the way, as well at the end. As Andy Andrews says in *Mastering The Seven Decisions That Determine Personal Success*: "Be on the lookout for something that will change everything" - for others and for yourself.

12. Tutor Students

You're not always expected to have a degree to help out. If you do, all the better. Check with your local public and private schools.

13. Try To Keep Your Patience - And Don't Try Any Either

It's easy to get aggravated. I've done it plenty. When someone aggravates you, try to think of what John Watson said: "Be kind – everyone is fighting a hard battle."

Try to emulate the patience of counselors who listen to other people's problems every day, helping them get back on track, all when they have problems of their own like the rest of us. If they can have patience all day, we should try to have it a little longer than usual. It can help to remember to: "Love our crooked neighbor with all our crooked heart." Others aren't perfect. Neither are we.

Watch your own behavior so you don't aggravate anybody else either. You won't be alone. I am working on that too. "Discourtesy does not spring from one bad quality, but from several – foolish vanity, from ignorance of what is due to others, from indolence, from stupidity, from distraction of thought, from contempt for others, from jealousy." - Jean de La Bruyere

14. Go Through Your Closets

If you have anything in your closets you haven't worn in the last year, give it away. Drop it off at a homeless shelter or take it to a thrift shop where it can help assist the less fortunate. New packages of underwear and socks are often needed at homeless shelters. Donate any coats and sweaters you don't need. Don't let someone else be cold on a dark, windy winter night when there are unused coats and sweaters taking up space in your closets. It's amazing how much space can get freed up in a closet too when a few of the coats come out of there.

15. Help Clean Up After A House Party

When you're at an informal get together, whenever you get up, look around and quietly pick up some plates, napkins and empty beverage containers you see lying around and put them in the sink or trash. It simplifies the cleanup later. Ask your hosts to let you help cleanup at the end of the evening. Everybody knows what a drag cleanup can be before going to bed, or worse, having to face a disgusting mess the next morning.

16. Help Anybody Stuck For Money

Give what you can to help. When they thank you, tell them they'll have a chance to do the same for somebody else someday. From *More Random Acts of Kindness:* "I arrived at the airport in Pullman, Washington, excited about my approaching interview for admission to the University of Washington's veterinary school. I went directly to the rental car agency to pick up my car, only to find…that my credit card had been refused and I had no other means of payment. I ran to the pay phone and called my roommate back in California. I was trying to explain what had happened, in between hysterical sobs, when a man walked up to me, tapped me on the shoulder, handed me a hundred-dollar bill, and walked away. Thanks to the generous compassion of a total stranger, I made the interview on time and was accepted into the veterinary school." And all the animals she has helped since add their thanks too!

17. Take Visitors Where They Need To Go

When visiting Paris, my partner and I took the Metro to Montmartre to see the area and the Sacre Coeur Basilica. Its front steps offer stunning views of Paris. As dominant of a building as it is, I thought it would be obvious where it was, once we exited the Metro station. It wasn't. I asked an elderly lady which direction it was in. She didn't speak any English, and my "French" is pathetic, but she gestured for us to follow her. She led us down the street about three blocks to a point where the church was clearly visible. I nodded and thanked her, but she motioned insistently several times that we continue to follow her. We went about twenty more steps and she gestured with her hand for us to look up. Before us was a stunning, carpet of green grass and an unobstructed view of the basilica she wanted us to see, one we would have missed if we hadn't continued to follow her. We thanked her and then she turned and went on her way, down the same little street she had probably walked for decades before. She wouldn't settle for doing a partial kindness, but only the fullest one she could offer. Such sweetness and concern for strangers for us to emulate.

18. Hold The Door

Look behind you whenever you open a door and hold it for the next person. Most people appreciate it. It's an easy way to remind ourselves that kindness knows no exceptions, because as we go through life we'll have the opportunity to do this for people of all races, ages and ethnic backgrounds, from every station in life.

My mother told me that she had held the door for a bearded, young man who she described in the jargon of the Sixties, as looking like a "beatnik." He said, "Thanks a lot lady. You didn't have to do that." She said, "I was glad to. Why wouldn't I?" She said he was shocked beyond belief that a woman in her sixties would hold a door open for him.

I have had some occasions when someone simply breezes through a held door saying nothing. It used to annoy me, but now I look for the act to carry its own benefit, whether it's acknowledged or not. Remember this when any kind act you've done goes unacknowledged. Forget it. You've done a good thing. That's the best thanks you can get.

19. Improve The Lives of The Elderly And The Disabled

If you see anything you can do to help them, just ask. Show respect by honoring their response. I used to frequently see an elderly man in a North Jersey neighborhood where I lived who had difficulty walking. He carried a milk crate. He'd walk about twenty steps, then sit down on the crate. He was always walking alone. After watching this for months, I went up to him one day, excused myself, and asked him if he would mind if I got him one of those canes that can also be converted into a seat. He was very resolute and to the point saying that he didn't want one. I apologized for disturbing him, he thanked me, I bid him a good day and left.

It might have helped him, but he didn't want it for reasons of his own - and that was that. Sometimes you have to take a risk in an effort to try to help someone else. Most of the time, I've found that the risk bore fruit and the receiver welcomed the help. Sometimes, as in the case with the gentleman above, you might get it wrong as I did, and you're going to be rebuffed. It's a small price to pay to be able to do some worthwhile things. At least you won't have to wonder whether you should have said something or not.

In *My Father's People: A Family of Southern Jews*, author Louis Rubin, Jr. talks about his Aunt Dora, who lived her life in Charleston, South Carolina. She worked over fifty years, mainly as a legal secretary, although she had also been a part time hairdresser to make ends meet. She took up tap dancing in her fifties and continued doing it into her eighties. When she retired, she lived in an apartment overlooking the water. Her nephew gave her binoculars so she could scan her surroundings from her lofty perch. Her law firm gave her a marine radio so she could listen to the transmissions from the harbor traffic. She died in her mid-nineties.

These were thoughtful and innovative gifts because they added to his aunt's life. The lives of many seniors, and the homebound at any age, can be lonely and empty. What can you do to help make the life of a senior citizen, or someone who is home bound, more fulfilling? Maybe you could give of your time to visit them or take them somewhere, even if it is just out to the park to see people, the sun and the birds. Maybe you could do it regularly, maybe just sometimes, or maybe it's just not you. What about buying them something, or showing them something, that could make their hours happier, either in addition to, or instead of visiting? The gifts that Aunt Dora received added to her life. She probably felt appreciated, and thought of the givers' kindnesses many times as she used them over the years.

What kind of similar gift can you think of that would help add to someone's life? How about putting a bird feeder outside a window or door and giving a basic, birding picture book so someone can try to recognize what feathered friends have come to visit that day?

A single man I know took his mother in after her husband died when she could no longer be left alone. He easily could have let her go to a care facility, but instead he cooked for her, made sure she took all her medications, took her for all her medical appointments and to get her hair done, and kept her company for over two years. We have all probably heard of many women who have done this, but there are few men who do so on a daily basis unassisted. I told him many times that I thought he was a model for how someone should take care of a parent. [There obviously are times when this can't be done for a variety of reasons.] He'd just say simply and humbly: "Hey, she's my Mom."

Think of what you might be able to do to make someone's years of confinement or limited mobility more pleasurable. If the people I've mentioned could do what they did, maybe we can find one small thing to do to help some senior or disabled person who needs it.

What about giving someone a basic computer, even a used one, and providing a brief lesson on how to get on the internet and use it to get news or to send e-mails? Many older people have an aversion to computers, thinking it's too complicated or that they would never get it. They don't need to know how to be programmers, but just to learn a few basics. What a great gift of self for grandchildren to give their grandparents some elementary computer lessons. What would be more gratifying than having a grandchild who could teach a grandparent how to use a computer, enabling them to e-mail back and forth to each other? Just showing someone a few basics could open up a whole world of information, music, home shopping and potential friendships for those who have a limited life.

What about matching students with seniors to provide visitors, and to show that there are still people who care about them? Some schools do this already through social service clubs. What about yours? Not only does it help those in need, it can provide marvelous, eye opening insight for younger people.

20. Lighten The Load

Bring food, baked goods or a useful item to cheer up a friend or to help those at home during a hospitalization or after a death. Cut the grass, trim the hedges and shovel the driveway and sidewalk if they need it. Offer to paint inside or out, provide minor repairs and improvements and plant some flowers or shrubs.

Another great help is to pay for someone's lawn cutting, hedge trimming and yard cleanup services. It can give a widow, a recent divorcee, a senior or the home-bound a real boost, and take a burden off their mind, when they see that their property is well maintained. They have enough problems without being depressed by the fact that the outside of the property is getting away from them. Lighten an already heavy load. "It is always in the service of others that you find the bliss you are seeking."

21. Get Someone Out of A Scrape Or A Drenching

Get someone out of a scrape. Buy three cans of spray de-icer. Offer to spray someone's windshield when they're trying to scrape off the morning frost. It takes seconds and people love it! Surprisingly, many people will ask, "What is that? Where did you get it?" Like it came from Mars or something. Just give them one of yours. You have extras!

When you see some umbrellas on sale cheap, pick up a few and keep them in your car. When you see somebody getting drenched, just take one from your car or briefcase and give it to them. You - the producer of instant desiccation and happiness!

22. Free Ride

Pay the toll for the car behind you, if it looks as if the occupant could use a lift.

23. Cell Phone Help

Use your cell phone to call for help for those who seem as if they could use it or to report any unsafe situations you notice. Donate a cell phone you no longer need to businesses and organizations that reprogram them so that women can use them to protect themselves against domestic violence.

24. Say Cheese

Whenever you see someone taking a picture of his/her partner, or of someone taking a picture of a whole group, ask if you can take it for them. It's nice to have a special memory with both people, or everybody, in the shot. You'll probably get about a 70% acceptance rate. People appreciate it. Even those who decline will thank you for the offer.

25. Give It Up

Ever go to the movies alone? I had my seat on the end all picked out in a row of four. The seat next to me was empty. The other two on the inside were already occupied. Two older ladies came in just before the show started trying to find two seats together. I said to one of the ladies: "Here, take this one. I only need one." The lady said, "Oh thank you, you're so kind." Then I realized I was on to something! A few weeks later, I tried it again when I saw a lady searching for two. They were equally appreciative. I enjoyed the movies from my second locations just as well and felt like I helped somebody else. The effort was next to nothing. I'm having a hard time straightening out my neck though.

There are other opportunities to do similar things: let people in when they are stuck on a side street trying to get on to a busier highway or let someone go ahead of you in the checkout line.

26. Become Noteworthy

There's something about a note that can sometimes make it even more effective than a call or visit. It also shows a particular civility that has become a dying art, particularly in an era of e-mails.

A note allows the recipient to read it, and re-read it, in his/her own time. There are many opportunities: notes of appreciation, encouragement, congratulations, condolence, and just telling someone how special they are. Buy a box of plain quality notes so they can function in a multi-purpose capacity and will be available on a moment's notice. It's also nice to send a note with something on it you think the recipient will like. Keep some stamps in the note box, so the note writing or mailing won't be delayed for want of a stamp.

Notes of condolence hold a special place. Our funeral customs in the United States typically involve people calling on the family at a funeral home or house of worship. Families are inundated with condolences within a period of a few days, but they drop off sharply after the funeral. Send a note a few weeks later. It will get the recipient's full attention and give them something tangible to read and a remembrance of your thoughtfulness.

Write from the heart, just the way you would speak to the person, as if he/she were sitting in front of you. The thoughts below might be helpful:

- Time does not obliterate a sad memory, but it lessens the sting after a while. The pain doesn't disappear, it just becomes transformed somehow into an improved perspective
- The cream rises to the top. As time passes, the good memories come into clearer focus and help depress the sad ones.
- Prayer can help. For those who believe in prayer, it can be a great support in times of trial, and help you feel that you're not alone.
- If you, and the person you're writing to, believe in an afterlife, mentioning that a deceased loved one will be seen again can also help. The person who died might simply be viewed as having "gone

ahead", as Benjamin Franklin said in a letter of condolence he wrote to a relative. As he noted, some are called before others for reasons unknown to us, but eventually we all will follow, as "a place at the table" has already been set for us too.

Just open up your heart, using some, none or all of these sentiments that you feel to be appropriate, combined with any personal thoughts and encouragements.

27. Visit Nursing Home Residents

Great amounts of loneliness can reside here. Staff members at such facilities can tell you about residents who rarely get visitors – and not always because they don't have any relatives or friends who could come. Some never get any visitors at all. The elderly love to reminisce. There can be mutual benefit. You are lending a caring ear, but may also gain a friend, and much from the perspective of someone farther down the track of life than you are. It can help to keep a harried life and our own problems in proper perspective.

28. Make A Child Happy

Ever notice how easily children smile? Giving a child a little gift or even just making a funny face can bring laughter to children. As harness racing trainer Robbie Siegelman said: "If you can make a kid smile, I don't see why you wouldn't do it." – *USA Today/Reader's Digest*

29. Join A Support Group

You might have much more to offer than you think. As Rick Warren points out in *The Purpose Driven Life:* "Your most effective ministry will come out of your deepest hurts."

Your experience as a mother or father who has lost a child, parent or close friend, a breast cancer or disease survivor, widow, divorcee, veteran, survivor of drug, alcohol or sexual abuse, or as one affected by other burdens of life, can put you in a unique position to give others the experienced insight, courage and support they need.

We often wonder why we have to go through certain trials in life. Saint Francis said that: "Every moment has a dignity worth understanding." The better we understand, the more it can help us to obtain relief from our own pain through being open to helping others.

Let your own problems or tragedy make the road easier for someone else. As willing as people may be to help those with problems, few can help someone better than those who have already experienced them. Those facing such problems now are far more likely to listen to, and to be comforted by, someone else who has already walked a similar path.

30. Volunteer

Select something that interests you or something you can use your specialized talents for. Habitat for Humanity uses the skills of volunteers, sometimes very modest, to provide housing for those who cooperate in helping to provide housing for themselves.

Outreach programs to provide assistance in many ways are provided by synagogues, churches and other social organizations. Even if you don't feel you have any special talents, an organization will probably find a place you will fit well and will provide you with any necessary training.

Volunteering in a hospital can involve many different opportunities to serve, from working in the Admissions Office to interacting with patients. Many organizations will also permit you to switch positions, to add breadth and variety to the experience, and will be willing to adjust to the amount of time you can offer and to schedule you at suitable times.

There are organizations to assist the less fortunate, those with dependencies, the environment, animals and many others. One can help prepare or deliver meals, or serve as a volunteer at a food bank or thrift shop. Purchasing from them can help provide financial support in their service of the less fortunate.

Volunteering can also be an aid to healthful living. *US News and World Report* in "50 Ways To Fix Your Life" said: "For years, studies have shown what do-gooders have sensed all along: Volunteering doesn't just help people on the receiving end, it drastically improves the health and happiness of the givers too. A life with purpose is an energized life. Elderly volunteers demonstrated a decrease in depression and an improvement in overall physical health, and they live longer than their non-volunteering peers according to a University of Michigan study."

Volunteering is one of the best ways people over 60 can contribute to their own well being too, says Linda Fried, Director of the Center on Aging and Health at Johns Hopkins University. In a study she conducted...she found that 50% of her sample group grew strong enough to stop using canes within two years after joining a tutoring program...

Volunteer work also helped teens build valuable self-esteem and socialization skills. These results were found when volunteers gave at least 15 hours a week and did something that was meaningful to them.

John Tesh in *Intelligence For Your Life* points out a side advantage of joining together to help others: "If you're single and looking forward to meeting someone, imagine the type of person you'd meet in an organization that helps others." Although service by its nature expects no reward, the world has a way of returning it in many ways, sometimes in highly unexpected ones.

Banding together to make good things happen can produce beneficial effects far in excess of what we might be able to accomplish alone. As I sat watching The Philadelphia Orchestra at the beautiful Kimmel Center in Philadelphia one night, I was struck by what an analogy there was to good people joining together to help others. Each musician in the orchestra was talented in his/her own right, but by working together, they produce a synergy that never would be possible if they played individually, as talented as each of them are. I saw one hundred plus musicians with a combined total of hundreds of years experience producing a magnificent result brought about by a combination of focus, expertise and masterful direction. Helping others, with others, works the same way.

31. Carry Useful Things

Carry some helpful things with you: a few band-aids, a safety pin, a pack of matches, extra pens, a spare handkerchief, some tissues and any other odds and ends you might think of that somebody could use in a pinch. They can all fit nicely in a small leather case or change purse, or even a sealable sandwich bag. This all might sound a bit silly, but if someone needs a little something, you can help them deal quickly with a minor crisis, so they can get back on track again. They'll appreciate it. The little things...

32. Donate Books

As the United Negro College Fund's ads used to say so powerfully: "A mind is a terrible thing to waste." So is a worthwhile book. Make extra space in your home, or reduce the burden of moving, by passing on books you've read. Think of who could use your books, such as libraries who don't have much of a selection or those who could just use more books. It might be a local town library, a high school library, a community college library, or even those in other areas. It's fairly cheap to ship a whole carton of books, so if you hear about a library in another part of the country that could use some good books, perhaps you can help them.

33. Give Your Voice To Reading

Inquire about making tapes for the visually impaired or read to someone who is blind or has limited sight.

34. Organ Donation

Organ donation is a great way to help others. Let your wishes be known to your family and write out your preferences with respect to the taking of all or certain specified organs on appropriate forms.

The Today Show told a bittersweet story about a fine young man, whose father was a police officer. His son suffered an emotional upset and broke into his father's gun cabinet and barricaded himself into the family home. He accidentally dropped the 9mm handgun he was holding and was killed. In spite of the unbelievable grief his family felt at his passing, they agreed to allow his organs to be donated. A number of months later, his family received notification that their son's organs had benefited many people in a number of states. Whether facing a personal tragedy, or making a definitive statement while you still can, let your organs, or those of a loved one, make a difference in the lives of others.

35. Know How To Be Kind

A Gentile once asked the famed Rabbi Hillel what the essence of Torah was. He responded: "That which is hateful to you, do not do to your neighbor" [Quoted from Rambam's Ladder]. A corollary of that might be: "Think what you would like to have someone do for you, then go do it for others." Whatever you have needed or appreciated, someone else would welcome too, particularly if it meets a critical need.

36. Reach Out And Touch Someone

This was a theme for a telephone company many years ago. When we can't be there in person, we can still help others with a call or e-mail, offering support and a sympathetic ear.

Reaching out and touching someone can also be taken literally. Touch is probably the most overlooked sense, but it has great power. Naturally, it's very important that the person who would be touched would welcome and appreciate it. It can cause discomfort and just make things uncomfortable if it's not.

Touch can make a real comforting difference, whether

it's a hug or just a gentle hand on someone's arm. As Joel Osteen notes: "Somebody needs your hug today. Somebody needs your love. Somebody needs to feel your touch. You may not realize it, but there is healing in your hands. There is healing in your voice." Share your touch, your love and your voice with those who you know who need it.

37. Relieve A Caregiver

There are few groups of people who serve as faithfully as caregivers. Caregivers to the sick, dying and disabled often serve without relief, frequently to the detriment of their own physical and mental health. To provide occasional help to a caregiver can provide someone with private time and an opportunity to recharge.

Gordon Livingston, author of *Too Soon Old, Too Late Smart*, sums it up accurately when he speaks about parents, spouses and children who serve as caregivers for those disabled by Alzheimer's, schizophrenia or developmental handicaps: "Most medals for heroism are awarded for brief occasions in which people behaved bravely. Those who, day in and day out, care for a loved one are seldom recognized but have, in my mind, earned a special place in whatever heaven there may be."

38. Forgive

Forgiving someone may help them, but it helps you more. It may be difficult to forget, but when we don't forgive, more often than not the other person is just sailing along with life not giving a thought to the situation, while we remain partially or substantially immobilized. As Piero Ferrucci notes in *The Power of Kindness:* "Such is the state of no forgiveness:

stagnating rancor generating new rancor, and thus blocking vital energy, cramping thought, poisoning life." Let it go. We only hurt ourselves by carrying hurt. I've done it myself. Being rid of it is a whole lot better. Try it. Ferrucci states further that low forgivers show higher measurements of stress. The high forgivers had fewer health problems and had seen their doctors less frequently. Another study he cited indicated that forgiveness also promotes physical and mental health.

39. Follow Your Instincts

One of the best guides to kindness is simply to follow your instincts because that's probably where some of your callings may lie and also where you might be most likely to be effective. "Become a giver. Ask yourself often: What can I give here; how can I be of service to this person, this situation?" - [*The New Earth* -Eckhart Tolle]

"Life is not measured by the breath we take, but by the moments that take our breath away." What takes yours away? Seeing a child learn how to read, comforting a sick or dying person, saving a forest or historical building, seeing how you make a difference in your child's life…"Happy is he who bears a god within and obeys it." – Louis Pasteur

40. Stay Humble

We all have talents that can make us large in something. We should work our level best at whatever that is. It's important though that our largeness be accomplished inside the framework of humility.

It's easy to put more focus on ourselves and our ego than we should when we're the ones extending a kindness.

Similarly, in today's world, there's a real tendency to want to come out on top in what we do. But through humility in whatever we do, we are far more likely to find out who we are and be better directed to where we are going: "A humble person does not need to triumph in order to justify his existence. He knows well that some others are better than he is, and he accepts it. This elementary fact has huge consequences. If I do not try to be what I am not, I give myself permission to be what I am...To realize that we are not as important as we thought can be painful, but it is also liberating." - [*The Power of Kindness,* Piero Ferrucci]

When We Need Help

We all need help and support at some time in our life. While some of those occasions may be obvious to others, at other times, the only way we are going to get help is to ask for it. Having the good sense to ask for help when it's needed is a sign of strength, not weakness. It can make all the difference and keep us from sliding down any farther. Kindness is a two way street that usually requires the cooperation of the receiver. Don't get in the way of someone else's efforts to help you. Cooperate with kindness. Mutual benefit will be the reward.

Sometimes it might be difficult to find the help we need. What then? A long time priest prayed to God to let him win the lottery - joining many of the rest of us. He said: "God, I've served you faithfully for thirty five years. In return, don't you think I deserve to get the winning number just once?" A voice from heaven rang out saying: "Hey Father! Buy a ticket!" If we need help, praying might help, but we also have to do something to help ourselves. As Jonathan Winters commented: "If your boat doesn't come in, swim out to it.."

And While You're Waiting

While you're waiting, help somebody else. "There may be times when you cannot find help, but there is no time you cannot give help."- George Merriam. The best solution when we are burdened with a seemingly unsolvable problem or grief which seems to be too challenging for us to handle is to stay busy helping others or doing something else constructive. "There is release from anguish, in action" - Frank Lloyd Wright

Keeping Problems In Perspective

Robert Schuller offers a powerful remedy to help keep our own problems in proper perspective. He suggests one way to do this is to roll out "The Big N – Nevertheless", whenever necessary. "I just lost my job, nevertheless I still have my home, my health and a family that loves me." "My best friend just died, nevertheless she was a great friend to me for as long as I knew her."

A couple I know tragically lost their college age son suddenly when he died engaging in a sports activity. When I went to the viewing, I hugged his parents and told them how sorry I was. His father said, "We are really going to miss him, but we are thankful that we had him in our lives for nineteen years." It's not the first viewing I've been to where family members who have suffered a terrible loss have actually provided consolation to the callers. The resilience and positive viewpoint of some people is truly remarkable.

It can make us ashamed of the fuss we make over some of our own comparatively small problems.

> "..What will matter is every act of integrity, compassion, courage or sacrifice that enriched, empowered or encouraged others to emulate your example."
> -*What Will Matter* - Michael Josephson

Chapter 8

Make Someone Happy - And You Will Be Happy Too

Dale Carnegie, author of the classic best seller, *How To Win Friends and Influence People*, said we should try to make others so happy that "even the undertaker will be sorry when we die." Our kind, thoughtful manner and willingness to be there for others, can give us a permanent residence in the hearts of our family, friends and co-workers long after we have gone ahead.

It's all about "servant leadership", a management concept that should be honored more in the execution than the mention. The manager's job, and ours, is to provide the support and advice that's needed to help other's achieve their goals, and to serve as good role models, whether it's to meet new sales targets, to help someone find a job, to help them feed their children, or to find housing.

Keep Doing It Until You Get It Right

Sometimes, in retrospect, our efforts at kindness might not have been what we would have wanted. If it is still possible and sensible to act, just go back and try to do it better. I was walking down a street in Philadelphia and heard a low, meek voice from behind me saying: "Could you spare something for a veteran to get a cup of coffee?" It happened in an instant. I hadn't even noticed him as I passed him.

I turned and saw a man all stooped over. He told me he was a Vietnam Vet. I gave him a dollar and thanked him for his service. He said few people said that to him. I told him that even though many people were against the war that he had served his country. I gave him another dollar then I continued walking.

I crossed the street and somehow I wasn't satisfied with what I had done. I walked a few more steps and then just stopped. I thought: "Why don't you go back and try to do it right this time?" I walked back to the corner, crossed over and looked up the street for him. I walked up to him again handed him more and said: "You're not going to be able to get something decent to eat with what I gave you before." The kindness wasn't perfect, but I felt that by going back I had done a better job of it. Go back and do it again, whatever it is, if you have to.

I'm going to have to stop going to Philadelphia. Seriously, I am always glad to go there because it's a great place to visit. Later, I thought to myself: "I'm glad I gave that man something." Then, I realized I had it all wrong. He was the one that gave me something. Whenever we can help someone, with anything, they give us the privilege of not only being able to help them, but allow us to make ourselves more of what we can be and to get closer to seeing a fuller vision of ourselves.

Be Kind To Yourself

Psychologist Carl Yung remarked: "You cannot apply kindness and understanding to others, if you have not applied it to yourself." Take time to do things you like. Don't be doing for others all the time. It will only guarantee less than optimal performance and ultimately can lead to burn out. Some people think unless they keep at it all the time, they're shirking their duty and not doing their best. Randy Pausch [*The Last Lecture*] said that some of the best care giving advice they heard comes from flight attendants: "Put on your own oxygen mask before assisting others." He said he knew his wife would have to give herself permission to make herself a priority after he was gone. Maybe you need to give yourself permission too.

Both positive attitude and the ability to be helpful will be maximized if you take the time to regenerate your energy. In speaking of making investments, famed financier and advisor to presidents Bernard Baruch said: "No general should keep his troops fighting all the time." The same applies to any form of personally taxing kindness. Continuous performance isn't going to produce the same quality results, nor will it provide as sharp of a perspective, as performance with appropriate breaks and as extending kindness to yourself will.

Parents and grandparents can sometimes make this mistake, forgetting themselves and giving "everything" for their children or grandchildren, not leaving enough time for their own happiness, personal growth, and relationship development. The best gift parents can give their children is stability. Partners need to make private time for themselves and to get out alone frequently to keep their relationship vital.

Too much generosity, can also lead to self-centeredness and expectation that can undermine another's personal growth, so it needs to be selective and measured for the ultimate benefit of the recipient. Give appropriate amounts of help in any situation. No one learns how to fish when someone else keeps giving them fish.

Spending more time on kindness driven activity also requires good physical and mental health. Research has reinforced the fact that the ability to think, to perform and to problem solve improves with proper nutrition and proper rest.

If you can't seem to get it all done, think about these basics, and try to eliminate what's not essential, and delegate to others when you can, to free up more of your own time for higher-level activities. The excellent book, *Finding Your Own North Star* by Martha Beck, can be very helpful to busy women in reorganizing for a more personally meaningful and productive life. The broad message is equally meaningful for men: "To live a fulfilled life, take your lead from your essential self. If something causes stress and struggle, no matter how worthy it is, it's probably not your true direction. When you find something that gives you joy, and at which you seem easily productive, it is probably close to your North Star." I recommend this book highly. It would be a great gift for any woman who has too much on her plate or who could just use more help getting better organized.

Make Someone Happy - And You Will Be Happy Too

Give It Some Thought

How can you be kind and help others with the rest of your unfinished life and bring more happiness to your own life? Think about it, seek the advice of others whose wisdom you value, and if it's amenable to you, pray about it. With an active daily schedule, it's easy to keep pressing onward without giving much thought to how we might be able to make more of an impact. Create your own special niches.

The Six Perfections

Buddhist thought speaks of attaining the six perfections [Quoted from *The Dalai Lama's Little Book of Inner Peace*]. Defining them below in my own terms as they relate to kindness, they provide excellent benchmarks for what it takes to be kind:

- Generosity - Giving of our money, of our possessions and of ourselves
- Discipline - Kindness means disciplining ourselves to be attentive to opportunities for kindness and to be considerate in its practice
- Patience - It is a kindness to be patient. When we are helping people with their problems, they may not always be able to resolve them according to a time schedule we think is appropriate. It takes patience for us to give the time they need, instead of what we think the time frame should be. This can particularly apply to grieving. Many people recover in some reasonably predictable time frame. For others, it takes longer. It's not helpful to tell people to "get over it." Just be patient and keep trying to help and encourage them and suggest that they get professional if they're stuck.

- Effort - Kindness most often requires more than just being patient, it requires the extending of effort to help someone who needs it.
- Meditative Concentration - Kindness requires thinking about the impact we have on the world and what real, lasting legacy we're going to leave.
- Wisdom - Those who are kind will grow in wisdom, about people in general, and particularly about themselves.

The Proper Feel

Feel is important. If it feels right for you, it's probably what you should be doing. If it doesn't, look for something else. As Bernard Baruch commented: "Do what you do best and leave the rest to others." You are the playwright. Write your own script. Then play the part. Keep examining your performance and improving it.

"Do what you love, live at the hub, centered on your own bliss…Bliss is the track that has always been waiting for you with hidden hands, seeming to help you attract the right circumstances for the fulfillment of your work…Everyone has the right to become a hero of some kind." - Joseph Campbell. Heroes are those who finally discover who they are, then act accordingly. Exercising kindness can be a key that leads to that life-changing discovery.

The Character of Kindness

Kindnesses can be given at different levels. Some people extend the same type of kindness all of the time. Some kindnesses are given in expectation of something in return, some without expecting anything. Some kindness is open, sometimes it's anonymous. As Maimonides noted, kindness has different levels of purity. All of it can work together for good, with the varied kindnesses of others, to make a difference.

Maximize Your Impact By Joining With Others

Look at the difference a few mothers, who faced horrific circumstances with the loss of their children, made when they founded Mothers Against Drunk Driving [MADD], those who lobbied to pass Megan's Law to warn communities about sex offenders or John Walsh's creation of *America's Most Wanted* to assist in the apprehension of felons, after his own young son was kidnapped and murdered. The same strong characteristics that spurred efforts to fight against these evils can also be marshaled to foster the spread of kindness in something that you feel needs to be done.

Read More On Happiness and Kindness

Read some of the books and the websites mentioned at the end of the book. Share this book with others or get them a copy of their own. It can be a great gift for those who have been kind to you or for those who might benefit by learning more about creating a happier, more successful and kinder life for themselves and others.

Reiki Principles

Reiki is a method of natural healing. It contains a number of ethical principles. These precepts are consistent with sound advice, with many other philosophical and spiritual beliefs, and on point for our review of kindness:

- Just for today
- Do not anger
- Do not worry
  ["You worry all day, and what do you have to show for it." - *The Bible*]
- Be filled with gratitude
- Devote yourself to your work
- Be kind to all people

Focusing and Staying Unblocked

Another element in achieving what you seek is to develop a set of personal guidelines for yourself which you can use to measure any activities you are considering making a part of your overall happiness and helpfulness plan. It's also important to avoid obstacles to happiness, service and success. Charles Stanley of In Touch Ministeries has identified these as:

- Fear
- Doubt
- Excuses
- Procrastination
- Laziness
- Violation of Conscience
- Greed

Help your life to be fuller and happier by helping others live better lives. "You will never be truly fulfilled as a human being until you learn the simple secret of how to give your life away" – Joel Osteen.

Let it be said of you that you were last seen happy, doing good.

Chapter 9

Concluding Thoughts on Finding Happiness

"Happiness is the full use of your powers along the lines of excellence"
- John F. Kennedy, after the Greeks

There is general agreement among leading experts on happiness that attaching yourself to something higher can lead to happiness. This clearly makes kindness and selflessness an important potential avenue for achieving personal happiness. For many, it can help produce an improved life. This is not to suggest that this is the only route to happiness. We all have different interests and strengths and what would be a pre-eminent factor in one's life, may not play as important of a role in the lives of others. The main thing is to be true to yourself and to make your strengths an important part of what you do.

Being happier involves taking risks. If you feel as if something is missing, just remember that if you keep doing the same thing, you're going to keep getting the same unsatisfactory or lukewarm results. Making changes is an elemental part of becoming happier.

Risk is comparative. What seems like a great risk to us might pale in comparison to those faced by others. In *Take The Risk,* Ben Carson, a noted neurosurgeon from Johns Hopkins, describes the tremendous risks that were taken in separating conjoined twins. Few of us face the kind of risk that Carson and those patients and their families faced. It is highly instructive to read his story and to learn what tools he used to determine what a worthwhile risk is. His earlier years were far from indicative of the success he has achieved. It is a highly inspirational story for anyone, particularly someone who needs to rise above disadvantages to find success and happiness. It is also hard to imagine anyone providing more of a kindness to others than separating conjoined bodies to help affected patients lead normal lives.

The purpose of *Your Unfinished Life* was to specially highlight just one facet in the multi-faceted diamond of happiness. Emerson truly noted that: "We are what we think about all day long." No matter who we are, we seek happiness and satisfaction from what we do. In being more selective about what we do, and why we do it, we can find the happiness we seek for ourselves and others who are put in front of us.

I've read many excellent books on happiness and kindness. I pass the following on to you. Many of the thoughts they contain have been helpful to me. I believe they may be beneficial to you too.

Your comments, your thoughts on how this book has helped you, and examples of how kindness received has helped make a difference in your life, may be sent to the author at: helpfulmedia@yahoo.com. Have a good and happy life.

Resources

Identifying Personal Sources of Happiness

Authentic Happiness
Martin Seligman

Flow
Mihaly Csikszentmihalyi

The How of Happiness
Sonja Lyubomirsky

Happier
Tal Ben-Shahar

Your Best Life Now – 7 Steps To Living Life —At Your Full Potential
Joel Osteen

Psychological Insights into Happiness

Finding Meaning in the Second Half of Life
James Hollis

The Power of Kindness
Piero Ferrucci

Too Soon Old, Too Late Smart
Gordon Livingston

Capstone Reading

The Seven Habits of Highly Successful People
Stephen Covey

The Seven Spiritual Laws of Success
Deepak Choprah

The Last Lecture
Randy Pausch

A New Earth: Awakening To Your Life's Purpose
Eckhart Tolle

Additional Books

On Kindness
Jean Guibert

Kindness
Frederick W. Faber

10 Secrets For Success and Inner Peace
Wayne Dyer

Blink
Malcolm Gladwell

The Dalai Lama's Little Book of Inner Peace
The Dalai Lama

George Foreman's Guide To Life
George Foreman

The Giving Tree
Shel Silverstein

The Kindness of Strangers
Don George [Editor]

Living Faith
Jimmy Carter

Mastering The Seven Decisions that Determine Personal Success
Andy Andrews

Meditations
Marcus Aurelius

More Random Acts of Kindness
Conari Press

My Father's People, A Family of Southern Jews
Louis Rubin, Jr.

Power Thoughts
Robert Schuller

The Practice of Kindness
Conari Press

Rambam's Ladder
Julie Salamon

Random Acts of Kindness
Conari Press

The Right Words At The Right Time
Marlo Thomas

50 Self-Help Classics
Tom Butler-Bowdon

A Short Course on Kindness
Margot Silk Forrest

Take The Risk
Ben Carson, MD

The Way of The Small
Michael Gellert

The Working Poor
David Shipler

Websites

Amazon.com
www.amazon.com/books
A source for many books on happiness and kindness.

Kindness Inc.
www.kindness.org

Random Acts of Kindness Foundation
www.actsofkindness.org

Printed in the United States
151977LV00001B/102/P